Dillard's Presents

Southern Living

CHRISTMAS COOKBOOK

cooking · entertaining · giving

RONALD MCDONALD
HOUSE CHARITIES

benefiting Ronald McDonald House Charities

RONALD McDONALD
HOUSE CHARITIES

Merry Christmas

from all your friends at Dillard's.

We are proud to support the

Ronald McDonald House.

The purchase of this book helps families of seriously ill children have a comfortable haven near their child.

Thank you for your generosity.
May your family have a wonderful holiday season and a healthy and prosperous 2015.

CONTENTS

Give ubiquitous red poinsettias an updated twist by cutting the blossoms and tucking them into an ivy topiary. A vintage ice bucket makes an ideal container.

ARRANGE A FRESH TABLE

*For the holiday's prettiest centerpieces,
pair favorite serving pieces with an
abundance of fresh blooms.*

✦ Soup It Up ✦

Find creative uses for one-of-a-kind heirlooms or estate-sale finds,
such as this ironstone tureen.

Start With: A soup tureen.

The Big Idea: Large surfaces call for sizeable arrangements. Show off your cherished tureen with a robust floral display. It's just the right width and not too tall for guests to see over when seated. If you place this on a buffet table, make sure to incorporate the ladle and lid.

The Flowers: Curvy and often footed, tureens are perfect for pairing with equally voluptuous blooms. Our choice: white peonies.

They work great with the pictured English ironstone tureen and with a variety of china patterns and decorating styles. Fill with peony foliage, or use bay leaves or laurel from the garden.

The Details: Tuck in quinces or pears that have been spray-painted gold. (Try Krylon Premium 18 Kt. Gold Plate metallic spray paint.) Once the paint dries, skewer the end of the fruit with a wooden pick, and insert into the arrangement.

❖ Raise the Bar ❖

Ice buckets, such as this metal pineapple, make great vases because
they are often lined with plastic.

Start With: A decorative ice bucket.
The Big Idea: As long as your vessel
is watertight, it's fair game to use as a
vase. Repurposing an ice bucket is a
great ice breaker (pardon the pun) as
it's sure to get conversations going.
The Flowers: Don't save amaryllis
for the month of December—they're
available at florists and garden centers
now. Rather than red, opt for peachy
selections such as 'Faro' and 'Exotica.'
Mix with orange-and-yellow parrot
tulips, soft coral red standard tulips,
and ivory hypericum berries. Use
Japanese cryptomeria as the filler.
The Details: When the ice bucket
lid is as showy as this one, make it
part of the composition. Set to one
side, it can then be balanced with a
silver finger bowl filled with lemons,
limes, or nuts.

Pour on the Cream

Group similar pitchers together and fill with fresh-cut flowers for a simply beautiful decoration.

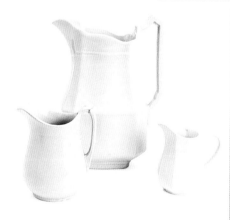

Start With: A trio of pitchers.

The Big Idea: Lots of food can leave little room for flowers. When space is tight, go vertical, saving valuable real estate for the most memorable part of the meal—dessert. Instead of filling that pitcher with tea, consider adding flowers. Try a trio in various heights.

The Flowers: Feature a different flower in each pitcher. To make arranging easy, use the largest bloom,

such as these white Oriental lilies, in the tallest pitcher. Add star of Bethlehem, lilies, and white pine to the middle pitcher. Then put chartreuse roses, green hypericum berries, and cedar or cypress in the shortest one.

The Details: Finish the look with satin ribbon and a mercury glass ball fit for decorating a tree.

Rise to the Occasion

Welcome guests in memorable Southern style with a duo
of bonbon compotes.

Start With: Two bonbon compotes.
The Big Idea: Twirl up topiaries with fruit.
The Flowers: Hot-glue sheet moss to a plastic-foam cone. Stick florist clay adhesive (joann.com) to the bottom of the compote, and press the cone onto it. Attach a row of green plums (or Key limes) by skewering with a wooden pick and inserting into the cone in an upward swirl. Glue scabiosa pods and dried hydrangea blossoms next. Repeat. Skewer a pineapple (spray-painted gold) with a wooden pick, and insert into top of topiary.

Florist Tip: Spray-paint the dried hydrangeas white. (We used Design Master Colortool Floral Spray paint in Flat White; joann.com).

⬥ Warm Up White ⬥

Create a topiary that belies its ease.

Start With: A silver casserole dish.

The Big Idea: Fast can be fabulous. To whip up a knockout arrangement that's ideal for any buffet, hold a bunch of lilies in your hand and wrap the stems with rubber bands.

Arrange It: Gather 8 to 12 stems of 'Casablanca' lilies in one hand, and cut stems so they're about 15 inches long. Wrap a rubber band around the stems at the top and another about 5 inches

from the bottom. Insert the bundle into the center of a water-soaked florist foam fitted into a casserole dish. Wrap stems with crisscrossed ribbon to hide the rubber bands. Add evergreens to the florist foam, and tie on ornaments with wire.

Florist Tip: Mix gold with silver. We layered two kinds of gold ribbon and then added large and small shiny and matte silver balls.

Punch Up the Color

Give your dining table a vivid focal point with a shiny punch bowl.

Start With: A silver punch bowl.

The Big Idea: Pair velvety red with chartreuse green to give the classic Christmas colors a fresh update.

The Flowers: Round shapes work best here. To make arranging easier in a wide container, use tape to make a grid across the top of the punch bowl. Add chartreuse-colored hydrangeas at each corner. Then add flowering cabbage toward the center and sides of the bowl, and pack in roses between the hydrangeas. Fill in with sprigs of red hypericum berries and white pine.

Florist Tip: Rotate the centerpiece to make sure it looks full from every angle. Add more hydrangeas, if needed.

MERRY STARTERS

Good friends and good food are a winning combination—especially during the holidays. This selection of appetizers and beverages makes any gathering more fun.

CRANBERRY-INFUSED
MOONSHINE

CRANBERRY-
MOONSHINE
COCKTAIL

FROZEN CRANBERRY-
MOONSHINE LEMONADE

CRANBERRY-INFUSED MOONSHINE

MAKES: about 3¼ cups • HANDS-ON TIME: 10 min. • TOTAL TIME: 15 min., plus 3 days for infusing

1 cup fresh cranberries
¼ cup sugar
1 (350-milliliter) bottle moonshine
2 (2- x 1-inch) orange rind strips

Cook cranberries, sugar, and 3 Tbsp. water in a saucepan over medium heat 5 minutes or until sugar dissolves, liquid begins to turn a light pink color, and cranberry skins begin to split. Let cool slightly (about 10 minutes). Pour mixture into a large glass jar; stir in moonshine and 2 (2- x 1-inch) orange rind strips. Let stand at room temperature 3 days. Pour through a fine wire-mesh strainer into a bowl; discard solids. Return moonshine mixture to jar. Store in refrigerator up to 2 months.

FROZEN CRANBERRY-MOONSHINE LEMONADE

MAKES: 5 cups • HANDS-ON TIME: 10 min. • TOTAL TIME: 10 min.

1 (12-oz.) can frozen lemonade concentrate
¾ cup sweet-and-spicy moonshine or Cranberry-Infused Moonshine
⅓ cup whole-berry cranberry sauce
2 Tbsp. orange liqueur
2 Tbsp. fresh lime juice

Combine lemonade concentrate, moonshine or Cranberry-Infused Moonshine, whole-berry cranberry sauce, orange liqueur, and fresh lime juice in a blender. Fill with ice to 5-cup level; process until smooth.

CRANBERRY-MOONSHINE COCKTAIL

MAKES: 1 serving • HANDS-ON TIME: 5 min. • TOTAL TIME: 5 min.

3 Tbsp. Cranberry-Infused Moonshine
1 Tbsp. orange liqueur
1 (25.4-oz.) bottle blood orange Italian soda, chilled

Combine 2 cups ice cubes, Cranberry-Infused Moonshine, and liqueur in a cocktail shaker. Cover with lid, and shake until chilled. Remove lid, and strain into a chilled glass; top with blood orange Italian soda. Serve immediately.

ULTIMATE ALEXANDER

One recipe fills the blender and will serve five to six people. Prepare two recipes to serve a party of 12.

MAKES: 5 cups ▪ **HANDS-ON TIME:** 5 min. ▪ **TOTAL TIME:** 5 min.

¼ cup cold brewed coffee
2 (14-oz.) containers coffee
ice cream
½ cup brandy
½ cup chocolate syrup
Garnishes: wafer cookies, whipped
topping, chocolate shavings

Process cold brewed coffee, ice cream, brandy, and chocolate syrup in a blender until smooth, stopping to scrape down sides. Pour mixture into glasses. Serve immediately.

Note: *We tested with Häagen-Dazs Coffee ice cream and Pepperidge Farm Chocolate Fudge Pirouette Rolled Wafers.*

CRAN-BOURBON-AND-ORANGE REFRESHER

MAKES: 1 serving ▪ **HANDS-ON TIME:** 5 min. ▪ **TOTAL TIME:** 5 min.

3 Tbsp. bourbon
1 Tbsp. Cranberry Reduction
1 Tbsp. fresh orange juice
Club soda
1 fresh rosemary sprig

Stir together bourbon, Cranberry Reduction, and fresh orange juice in a 10-oz. glass filled with ice cubes. Top with club soda and rosemary sprig.

Cranberry Reduction

MAKES: 1¼ cups ▪ **HANDS-ON TIME:** 10 min. ▪ **TOTAL TIME:** 2 hours, 5 min.

2 cups cranberry juice
½ cup canned jellied cranberry
sauce
¼ cup sugar
4 dashes of Angostura bitters
1 fresh rosemary sprig

Boil first 4 ingredients in a medium saucepan over medium heat, stirring often, 4 to 5 minutes or until smooth. Reduce heat to low, and simmer, stirring occasionally, 20 minutes or until liquid is reduced by half and slightly thickened. Add rosemary; cover and let stand 5 minutes. Discard rosemary. Cool mixture 30 minutes. Cover and chill 1 hour. Store in an airtight container in refrigerator for up to 1 week.

ULTIMATE ALEXANDER

CITRUS-MARINATED FETA
AND OLIVES

CITRUS-MARINATED FETA AND OLIVES

This gorgeous make-ahead dish is a crowd-pleaser at any gathering, and it's so easy to prepare.

MAKES: 6 to 8 servings ■ **HANDS-ON TIME:** 10 min. ■ **TOTAL TIME:** 10 min., plus 1 day for chilling

¼ cup chopped fresh basil
¼ cup olive oil
1 Tbsp. orange zest
1 tsp. coarsely ground pepper
1 garlic clove, minced
1 cup pitted kalamata olives
1 cup pimiento-stuffed
  Spanish olives
1 (8-oz.) feta cheese block, cubed

Whisk together first 5 ingredients in a medium-size glass bowl; gently stir in olives and cheese. Cover and chill 24 hours.

BARBECUE ROASTED NUTS

Two kinds of sugar sweeten this happy hour munchie. Buy shelled nuts to save time.

MAKES: 6 cups ■ **HANDS-ON TIME:** 30 min. ■ **TOTAL TIME:** 2 hours, 5 min.

2 large egg whites
2 lb. assorted whole, raw nuts,
  shelled
1 Tbsp. kosher salt
1 Tbsp. light brown sugar
2 tsp. smoked paprika
1½ tsp. granulated sugar
½ tsp. garlic powder
½ tsp. dry mustard
¼ tsp. ground cumin
¼ tsp. ground ginger

Preheat oven to 350°. Whisk egg whites in a large bowl until foamy; toss nuts with whites. Stir together salt and next 7 ingredients; sprinkle over nuts, and toss to coat. Arrange nuts in a single layer in a 17- x 11-inch jelly-roll pan; bake at 350° for 25 to 30 minutes or until toasted and fragrant, stirring occasionally. Cool on a wire rack (about 1 hour). Store in airtight containers for up to 1 week.

HOT SPINACH-ARTICHOKE DIP

MAKES: 8 servings • **HANDS-ON TIME:** 15 min. • **TOTAL TIME:** 45 min.

1 cup freshly grated Parmesan cheese
1 cup reduced-fat sour cream
½ cup mayonnaise
4 green onions, sliced
3 Tbsp. fresh lemon juice
1 garlic clove, pressed
1¼ cups (5 oz.) shredded pepper Jack cheese
1 (10-oz.) package frozen chopped spinach, thawed and drained
1 (14-oz.) can artichoke hearts, drained and chopped
Crackers
Assorted fresh vegetables

1. Preheat oven to 350°. Stir together first 6 ingredients and 1 cup pepper Jack cheese. Fold in spinach and artichokes. Spoon into a lightly greased 1-qt. baking dish. Sprinkle with remaining ¼ cup pepper Jack cheese.

2. Bake at 350° for 30 minutes or until center is hot and edges are bubbly. Add freshly ground black pepper to taste. Serve with crackers and assorted fresh vegetables.

ROQUEFORT CHEESECAKE
with Pear Preserves and Pecans

MAKES: 12 appetizer servings • **HANDS-ON TIME:** 15 min. • **TOTAL TIME:** 9 hours, 45 min.

2 (8-oz.) packages cream cheese, softened
1 (8-oz.) package Roquefort cheese, chopped
½ cup sour cream
2 Tbsp. chopped fresh chives
1 Tbsp. chopped fresh parsley
2 large eggs
2 Tbsp. all-purpose flour
½ (11.5-oz.) jar pear preserves
½ cup toasted pecan or walnut halves
Grapes

1. Preheat oven to 325°. Beat cream cheese and next 4 ingredients at medium speed with an electric mixer until blended. Add eggs, 1 at a time, beating just until yellow disappears; fold in flour. Spoon mixture into a lightly greased 7-inch springform pan.

2. Bake at 325° for 1 hour or until set. Run a knife around outer edge of cheesecake to loosen from sides of pan. Let cool in pan on a wire rack 30 minutes. Cover and chill 8 hours. Remove sides of pan. Transfer cheesecake to a platter, and spoon preserves over top; sprinkle with pecans. Serve with grapes.

ROQUEFORT CHEESECAKE

HOT SPINACH-
ARTICHOKE DIP

CHEESE RING

CHEESE RING
with Strawberry Preserves

MAKES: 8 to 10 servings ▪ **HANDS-ON TIME:** 20 min. ▪ **TOTAL TIME:** 2 hours, 20 min.

¾ cup mayonnaise
½ tsp. hot sauce
1 garlic clove, minced
1 cup finely chopped toasted pecans
2 (8-oz.) blocks sharp Cheddar cheese, finely grated*
½ cup strawberry preserves
Assorted crackers
Garnishes: chopped toasted pecans, fresh strawberries, strawberry flowers

1. Stir together mayonnaise and next 2 ingredients. Stir in pecans and cheese.

2. Spoon mixture into a plastic wrap-lined 4-cup ring mold with a 2 ½-inch center. Cover and chill 2 hours.

3. Unmold cheese ring onto a serving platter. Discard plastic wrap. Fill center of ring with preserves. Serve with crackers.

Sharp white Cheddar cheese may be substituted.

SUN-DRIED TOMATO MARINATED BOCCONCINI IN GARLIC OIL

MAKES: 7 half-pints ▪ **HANDS-ON TIME:** 17 min. ▪ **TOTAL TIME:** 17 min., plus 1 day for marinating

1 (7-oz.) jar sun-dried tomatoes in oil
1 cup olive oil
¾ cup white wine vinegar
1 Tbsp. fresh thyme leaves
1 tsp. freshly ground black pepper
¾ tsp. salt
5 garlic cloves, coarsely chopped
2 lb. bocconcini mozzarella, drained
7 (½-pt.) jars, sterilized

Drain tomatoes, reserving oil. Chop tomatoes. Process tomato oil, olive oil, and next 5 ingredients in a blender until smooth. Pour into a bowl; stir in chopped tomatoes. Add cheese, stirring to coat. Fill jars with cheese, and marinate in refrigerator at least 24 hours before serving. Store in refrigerator up to 1 week.

TORTELLINI CAPRESE BITES

Tortellini Caprese Bites, drizzled with a basil vinaigrette, are so simple to prepare. The no-mess presentation makes these appetizer skewers ideal for parties.

MAKES: 12 servings ▪ **HANDS-ON TIME:** 30 min. ▪ **TOTAL TIME:** 2 hours, 30 min.

1   (9-oz.) package refrigerated
    cheese-filled tortellini
3   cups halved grape tomatoes
3   (8-oz.) containers fresh small
    mozzarella cheese balls
60 (6-inch) wooden skewers
Basil Vinaigrette

1. Prepare tortellini according to package directions. Rinse under cold running water.

2. Thread 1 tomato half, 1 cheese ball, another tomato half, and 1 tortellini onto each skewer. Place skewers in a 13- x 9-inch baking dish. Pour Basil Vinaigrette over skewers, turning to coat. Cover and chill 2 hours. Transfer skewers to a serving platter, and add salt and pepper to taste. Discard any remaining vinaigrette.

Note: *We tested with Whole Foods Market Ciliegine Fresh Mozzarella Cheese.*

Basil Vinaigrette

MAKES: 1½ cups ▪ **HANDS-ON TIME:** 10 min. ▪ **TOTAL TIME:** 10 min.

½   cup white balsamic vinegar
1   tsp. kosher salt
⅔   cup extra virgin olive oil
6   Tbsp. chopped fresh basil

Whisk together vinegar and salt until blended. Gradually add oil in a slow, steady stream, whisking constantly until smooth. Stir in basil and freshly ground black pepper to taste.

HONEY-ROSEMARY CHERRIES AND BLUE CHEESE CROSTINI

MAKES: 8 appetizer servings ▪ **HANDS-ON TIME:** 20 min. ▪ **TOTAL TIME:** 30 min.

1   shallot, thinly sliced
2   tsp. olive oil
1   (12-oz.) package frozen dark,
      sweet pitted cherries, thawed
2   Tbsp. balsamic vinegar
2   Tbsp. honey
1/4   tsp. chopped fresh rosemary
1/8   tsp. salt
1/8   tsp. pepper
2   cups loosely packed arugula
16   (1/4-inch-thick) ciabatta bread
      slices, toasted
1   (8-oz.) wedge blue cheese,
      thinly sliced*

1. Sauté shallot in hot oil in a medium skillet over medium-high heat 2 to 3 minutes or until tender. Add cherries (and any liquid in package) and next 5 ingredients. Cook, stirring occasionally, 8 to 10 minutes or until thickened. Let stand 10 minutes.

2. Divide arugula evenly among toasted bread slices. Top each with cherry mixture and 1 blue cheese slice.

*Manchego or goat cheese may be substituted.

Begin your party casually by offering this appetizer "help yourself" style. Or make single-serving plates, and present them as a first course at the table.

PEPPER JACK-GRITS POPPERS

MAKES: about 10 appetizer servings ▪ **HANDS-ON TIME:** 35 min. ▪ **TOTAL TIME:** 8 hours, 40 min.

1   cup hot cooked grits
1   cup (4 oz.) freshly shredded
      pepper Jack cheese
½   cup shredded Parmesan cheese
2   Tbsp. chopped fresh cilantro
1   garlic clove, pressed
18 to 20 sweet mini bell peppers

1. Stir together first 5 ingredients until cheese melts; add salt and pepper to taste. Cover and chill 8 hours.

2. Preheat broiler with oven rack 6 inches from heat. Cut peppers in half lengthwise, leaving stems intact; remove seeds. Spoon grits mixture into pepper halves. Place on a broiler pan. Broil 4 minutes or until golden brown.

CHEESE-AND-BACON OKRA POPPERS

We loved the bacon-wrapped pods, but you can save prep time by crumbling the bacon into the cheese mixture, stuffing the pods, and baking.

MAKES: 16 servings ▪ **HANDS-ON TIME:** 20 min. ▪ **TOTAL TIME:** 44 min.

16   bacon slices
1   lb. fresh okra (32 pods)
1   (8-oz.) container chive-and-
       onion cream cheese, softened
½   cup shredded extra-sharp
       Cheddar cheese
¼   cup chopped green onions
¼   tsp. kosher salt
¼   tsp. freshly ground pepper
32 wooden picks
Vegetable cooking spray

1. Preheat oven to 425° with oven rack 6 inches from heat. Cook bacon, in 2 batches, in a large skillet over medium-high heat 1 to 2 minutes on each side or just until bacon begins to curl; remove bacon, and drain on paper towels. Cut each slice in half crosswise. Discard drippings.

2. Cut each okra pod lengthwise down 1 side, leaving stem and other side of pod intact; remove seeds and membranes.

3. Stir together cream cheese and next 4 ingredients in a small bowl. Carefully pipe cheese mixture into cavity of each okra pod. Wrap each stuffed okra pod with 1 bacon piece, and secure with a wooden pick.

4. Place half of okra, cheese side up, on a foil-lined baking sheet coated with cooking spray. Bake at 425° for 8 minutes or until okra is tender and bacon is crisp. Transfer to a serving platter; keep warm. Repeat procedure with remaining half of okra. Serve warm.

CHEESE-AND-BACON
OKRA POPPERS

PEPPER JELLY-PECAN RUGELACH

MAKES: about 5 dozen ▪ **HANDS-ON TIME:** 30 min. ▪ **TOTAL TIME:** 2 hours, 15 min.

2¼ cups all-purpose flour
1   cup cold butter, cut into pieces
1   (8-oz.) package cream cheese,
       cut into pieces
½   tsp. salt
1   (10-oz.) jar red pepper jelly
1   cup finely chopped
       toasted pecans
Parchment paper

1. Pulse first 4 ingredients in a food processor 3 or 4 times or until dough forms a ball and leaves sides of bowl. Divide dough into 8 portions, shaping each into a ball. Wrap each separately in plastic wrap; chill 1 to 24 hours.
2. Preheat oven to 375°. Cook pepper jelly in a small saucepan over medium heat, stirring often, 2 to 3 minutes or just until melted.
3. Roll 1 dough ball into an 8-inch circle on a lightly floured surface. Brush dough with 1 to 2 Tbsp. melted jelly; sprinkle with 2 Tbsp. pecans. Cut circle into 8 wedges, and roll up wedges, starting at wide end, to form a crescent shape. Place, point sides down, on a lightly greased parchment paper-lined baking sheet. Repeat procedure with remaining dough balls, pepper jelly, and pecans.
4. Bake at 375° for 15 to 20 minutes or until golden brown. Transfer to wire racks. Cool completely (30 minutes).

PLAN AHEAD

Make these crunchy treats ahead of time and serve at room temperature. They're a perfect holiday pickup food.

BACON-WRAPPED SHRIMP

MAKES: 2 dozen ▪ HANDS-ON TIME: 20 min. ▪ TOTAL TIME: 1 hour

24 unpeeled, large raw shrimp
¼   cup canola oil
¼   cup balsamic vinegar
3   Tbsp. chopped fresh basil
2   shallots, minced
1   garlic clove, minced
1   Tbsp. light brown sugar
¼   tsp. ground red pepper
⅛   tsp. salt
12 bacon slices, cut in half crosswise
24 wooden picks

1. Preheat oven to 450°. Peel and devein shrimp, leaving tails on. Combine canola oil and next 7 ingredients in a zip-top plastic freezer bag. Add shrimp; seal and chill 30 minutes, turning once.
2. Meanwhile, arrange bacon in a single layer in a 15- x 10-inch jelly-roll pan. Bake at 450° for 6 to 8 minutes or just until bacon begins to brown. (Bacon will be partially cooked, not crisp.) Remove from pan, and drain on paper towels. Reduce oven temperature to 400°.
3. Place a lightly greased wire rack in an aluminum foil-lined 15- x 10-inch jelly-roll pan. Remove shrimp from marinade; discard marinade. Wrap 1 bacon piece around each shrimp, and secure with a wooden pick threaded through both ends of shrimp. Arrange shrimp in a single layer on wire rack.
4. Bake at 400° for 8 to 10 minutes or until bacon is crisp and shrimp turn pink. Serve immediately.

BACON-WRAPPED BOURBON FIGS

MAKES: 2 dozen ▪ HANDS-ON TIME: 20 min. ▪ TOTAL TIME: 55 min.

12 dried Calimyrna figs
¼   cup bourbon
1   (2- to 4-oz.) wedge Gorgonzola cheese, cut into 24 pieces
24 pecan halves, toasted
12 fully cooked bacon slices, cut in half crosswise
24 wooden picks

1. Combine first 2 ingredients and 1½ cups water in a medium saucepan. Cook, covered, over low heat 15 to 20 minutes or until figs are plump and softened. Remove from heat; cool slightly (about 15 minutes). Drain figs; gently pat dry with paper towels.
2. Preheat oven to 350°. Cut figs in half lengthwise. Place 1 cheese piece and 1 pecan half on cut side of each fig half. Wrap 1 bacon piece around each fig, and secure with a wooden pick. Place on a wire rack in a 15- x 10-inch jelly-roll pan.
3. Bake at 350° for 6 to 8 minutes or until bacon is crisp and browned.

Note: *We tested with Oscar Mayer Fully Cooked Bacon.*

BACON-WRAPPED SHRIMP

BACON-WRAPPED
BOURBON FIGS

FINGERLING POTATOES
with Avocado and Smoked Salmon

MAKES: 8 servings ▪ **HANDS-ON TIME:** 15 min. ▪ **TOTAL TIME:** 55 min.

1 lb. fingerling potatoes,
   halved lengthwise
1 Tbsp. olive oil
½ tsp. salt
¼ tsp. pepper
1 ripe avocado, halved
1 Tbsp. minced fresh dill weed
1 tsp. lemon zest
2 tsp. fresh lemon juice
⅛ tsp. salt
1 (4-oz.) package thinly sliced
   smoked salmon
Garnish: fresh dill sprigs

1. Preheat oven to 400°. Toss together first 4 ingredients. Place potatoes, cut sides down, in a lightly greased jelly-roll pan. Bake at 400° for 20 minutes or until tender and browned. Cool completely (about 20 minutes).
2. Meanwhile, scoop avocado pulp into a bowl; mash with a fork. Stir in dill weed and next 3 ingredients. Spoon mixture onto cut sides of potatoes, and top each with 1 salmon slice.

You'll love the unexpected flavor combination of creamy avocado and fresh dill atop roasted potatoes.

PORK TENDERLOIN
CROSTINI

PEPPER JELLY-GOAT CHEESE
CAKES (PAGE 40)

PORK TENDERLOIN CROSTINI

MAKES: 4 dozen ▪ **HANDS-ON TIME:** 30 min. ▪ **TOTAL TIME:** 2 hours, 50 min., including Cranberry-Pepper Jelly

24 frozen tea biscuits
2 (¾- to 1-lb.) pork tenderloins
1 tsp. salt
2 tsp. freshly ground pepper
2 Tbsp. olive oil
5 Tbsp. butter, melted
Cranberry-Pepper Jelly
1 bunch fresh watercress

1. Preheat oven to 350°. Bake tea biscuits according to package directions. Cool on a wire rack 20 minutes.

2. Preheat grill to 350° to 400° (medium-high) heat. Remove silver skin from each tenderloin. Sprinkle salt and pepper over pork; rub with olive oil. Grill pork, covered with grill lid, 10 to 12 minutes on each side or until a meat thermometer inserted into thickest portion registers 145°. Remove from grill; cover with aluminum foil, and let stand 15 minutes.

3. Meanwhile, cut biscuits in half, and brush cut sides with melted butter. Arrange, cut sides up, on a baking sheet. Bake at 350° for 8 to 10 minutes or until edges are golden.

4. Cut pork into ¼-inch-thick slices (about 24 slices each). Place pork on biscuit halves; top with desired amount of Cranberry-Pepper Jelly and watercress sprigs. Serve immediately.

Cranberry-Pepper Jelly

MAKES: 3 cups ▪ **HANDS-ON TIME:** 25 min. ▪ **TOTAL TIME:** 1 hour, 10 min.

1 (12-oz.) package fresh cranberries
1 (10-oz.) jar red pepper jelly
1½ cups peeled and diced Granny Smith apple
¾ cup sugar
¼ tsp. dried crushed red pepper
½ cup sweetened dried cranberries

Bring fresh cranberries, jelly, apple, sugar, ½ cup water, and crushed red pepper to a boil in a large saucepan over medium-high heat, stirring often. Reduce heat to medium-low, and simmer, stirring often, 10 to 15 minutes or until cranberry skins begin to split and mixture starts to thicken. Remove from heat, and stir in sweetened dried cranberries. Cool completely (about 45 minutes). Serve at room temperature, or cover and chill 8 hours before serving. Store in an airtight container in refrigerator for up to 2 weeks.

PEPPER JELLY-GOAT CHEESE CAKES

(pictured on page 38)

MAKES: 2 dozen ▪ **HANDS-ON TIME:** 20 min. ▪ **TOTAL TIME:** 2 hours, 50 min.

24 aluminum foil miniature
    baking cups
Vegetable cooking spray
¼ *cup fine, dry Italian-seasoned*
    breadcrumbs
¼ *cup ground toasted pecans*
2 *Tbsp. grated Parmesan cheese*
2 *Tbsp. butter, melted*
1 *(8-oz.) package cream cheese,*
    softened
1 *(4-oz.) goat cheese log, softened*
1 *large egg*
2 *Tbsp. heavy cream*
1 *Tbsp. Asian hot chili sauce*
    (such as Sriracha)
¼ *cup green pepper jelly, melted*
¼ *cup red pepper jelly, melted*

1. Preheat oven to 350°. Place baking cups in 2 (12-cup) miniature muffin pans; coat baking cups with cooking spray.
2. Stir together breadcrumbs and next 3 ingredients. Firmly press about 1 tsp. breadcrumb mixture in bottom of each baking cup.
3. Beat cream cheese and goat cheese at medium speed with an electric mixer until light and fluffy; add egg and next 2 ingredients, beating just until blended. Spoon into baking cups, filling three-fourths full.
4. Bake at 350° for 10 minutes or until set. Cool completely in pans on a wire rack (about 20 minutes). Spoon 1 tsp. melted green pepper jelly over each of 12 cheesecakes. Spoon 1 tsp. melted red pepper jelly over each of remaining 12 cheesecakes. Cover and chill 2 to 12 hours before serving.

Tip: To melt pepper jellies, microwave them in a microwave-safe bowl at HIGH for 20 to 25 seconds.

SHRIMP AND CITRUS COCKTAIL

Give this updated classic a fresh look by serving it in modern stemmed glassware.

MAKES: 4 to 6 servings ▪ **HANDS-ON TIME:** 15 min. ▪ **TOTAL TIME:** 3 hours, 15 min.

1 *lb. peeled, large cooked*
    shrimp with tails
⅓ *cup olive oil*
⅓ *cup red wine vinegar*
2 *large shallots, minced*
2 *tsp. Dijon mustard*
2 *tsp. orange zest*
½ *tsp. salt*
½ *tsp. dried crushed red pepper*
2 *large navel oranges, peeled*
    and sectioned
3 *Tbsp. chopped fresh basil*

1. Devein shrimp, if desired.
2. Whisk together olive oil and next 6 ingredients in a large bowl. Pour mixture into a large zip-top plastic freezer bag; add shrimp, turning to coat. Seal and chill 3 to 8 hours, turning occasionally. Remove shrimp from marinade; discard marinade. Combine shrimp, oranges and basil. Spoon mixture into chilled glasses or small serving bowls.

SHRIMP AND CITRUS
COCKTAIL

SALT-ROASTED BEEF TENDERLOIN SLIDERS

MAKES: 8 servings ▪ **HANDS-ON TIME:** 20 min. ▪ **TOTAL TIME:** 1 hour, 25 min.

1 (1½-lb.) beef tenderloin, trimmed
1 tsp. cracked pepper
1 Tbsp. olive oil
6 cups kosher salt
1 cup cold water
24 small rolls or buns, split and toasted
Chimichurri Pesto
4 plum tomatoes, thinly sliced

1. Preheat oven to 400°. Sprinkle beef with pepper. Cook in hot oil in a skillet over medium-high heat, turning occasionally, 5 minutes or until browned on all sides.

2. Stir together salt and 1 cup cold water. Spread half of salt mixture in a rectangle (slightly larger than beef) in a large roasting pan; top with beef. Pat remaining salt mixture over beef, covering completely.

3. Bake at 400° for 45 to 50 minutes or until a meat thermometer inserted into center registers 145°. Remove crust. (Beef will keep cooking if crust remains on.) Transfer beef to a cutting board. Cover loosely with aluminum foil; let stand 10 minutes. Brush off excess salt; slice beef. Serve beef in rolls with pesto and sliced tomatoes.

Chimichurri Pesto

MAKES: about 1 cup ▪ **HANDS-ON TIME:** 10 min. ▪ **TOTAL TIME:** 10 min.

1 cup firmly packed fresh flat-leaf parsley leaves
1 cup firmly packed fresh cilantro leaves
½ cup chopped toasted walnuts
½ cup freshly grated Parmesan cheese
1 tsp. fresh lemon juice
1 small garlic clove, chopped
¼ tsp. salt
¼ tsp. dried crushed red pepper
¼ cup extra virgin olive oil

Process parsley leaves, cilantro leaves, walnuts, Parmesan cheese, fresh lemon juice, garlic, salt, and red pepper in a food processor until finely chopped. With processor running, pour olive oil through food chute in a slow, steady stream, processing until smooth.

SEASONAL SIDES & SALADS

Round out your meal with these colorful and tasty dishes. From classic mashed potatoes to green beans with a twist, there's something for every occasion.

CRISPY GOAT CHEESE-TOPPED ARUGULA SALAD

MAKES: 8 servings ▪ **HANDS-ON TIME:** 25 min. ▪ **TOTAL TIME:** 1 hour, 50 min., including vinaigrette

4   (4-oz.) goat cheese logs
½   cup all-purpose flour
½   tsp. freshly ground black pepper
2   large egg whites
1   cup panko (Japanese breadcrumbs)
4   Tbsp. olive oil
2   (5-oz.) containers baby
        arugula
4   large navel oranges, peeled
        and sectioned
Pomegranate Vinaigrette
Garnish: pomegranate seeds

1. Cut each goat cheese log into 6 (½-inch-wide) slices. Combine flour and black pepper in a shallow dish. Whisk together egg whites and 2 Tbsp. water in another shallow dish. Place panko in a third shallow dish. Dredge goat cheese in flour mixture, dip in egg mixture, and dredge in panko. Arrange goat cheese in a single layer in an aluminum foil-lined jelly-roll pan; cover and chill 30 minutes to 4 hours.

2. Cook half of goat cheese rounds in 2 Tbsp. hot oil in a large nonstick skillet over medium heat 2 to 3 minutes on each side or until lightly browned; drain on paper towels. Repeat with remaining oil and goat cheese rounds.

3. Divide arugula and orange sections among 8 plates; drizzle with Pomegranate Vinaigrette. Top each salad with 3 goat cheese rounds.

Tip: To get clean slices of cheese, dip the knife in hot water.

Pomegranate Vinaigrette

MAKES: ⅔ cup ▪ **HANDS-ON TIME:** 20 min. ▪ **TOTAL TIME:** 55 min.

1½   cups pomegranate juice
⅓   cup olive oil
5   tsp. honey
1   Tbsp. white wine vinegar
1   tsp. Dijon mustard
¼   tsp. freshly ground black pepper

Bring 1½ cups pomegranate juice to a boil in a medium saucepan over medium-high heat; reduce heat to medium, and cook, stirring occasionally, 15 minutes or until reduced to ¼ cup. Transfer to a small bowl. Cool completely (about 30 minutes). Whisk in oil and next 4 ingredients. Add salt to taste.

ARUGULA-PEAR-BLUE CHEESE SALAD

MAKES: 8 servings ▪ HANDS-ON TIME: 15 min. ▪ TOTAL TIME: 15 min.

¼ cup pear preserves
½ cup Champagne vinegar
1 shallot, sliced
2 tsp. Dijon mustard
½ tsp. table salt
¼ tsp. freshly ground black pepper
½ cup olive oil
2 Tbsp. pear preserves
8 cups loosely packed arugula
2 Bartlett pears, cut into
   6 wedges each
4 oz. blue cheese, crumbled
¼ cup chopped toasted walnuts

1. Process ¼ cup preserves and next 5 ingredients in a food processor 30 seconds to 1 minute or until smooth. With food processor running, pour oil through food chute in a slow, steady stream, processing until smooth. Transfer to a 2-cup measuring cup or small bowl, and stir in 2 Tbsp. pear preserves.
2. Place arugula in a large serving bowl. Top with pears, blue cheese, and walnuts. Drizzle with vinaigrette.

HERBS AND GREENS SALAD

MAKES: 6 to 8 servings ▪ HANDS-ON TIME: 10 min. ▪ TOTAL TIME: 30 min.

½ tsp. lemon zest
4 Tbsp. olive oil, divided
3 cups 1-inch olive bread cubes*
4 cups torn butter lettuce
   (about 1 head)
2 cups firmly packed fresh baby
   spinach
1 cup torn escarole
½ cup loosely packed fresh
   parsley leaves
¼ cup fresh 1-inch chive pieces
2 Tbsp. fresh lemon juice

1. Preheat oven to 425°. Stir together lemon zest and 1 Tbsp. olive oil in a large bowl. Add bread cubes, and toss to coat. Arrange in a single layer on a baking sheet. Bake at 425° for 5 minutes or until crisp. Cool completely (about 15 minutes).
2. Meanwhile, combine butter lettuce and next 4 ingredients in a large bowl. Drizzle with lemon juice and remaining 3 Tbsp. olive oil, and toss to coat. Add salt and pepper to taste. Serve immediately with toasted bread cubes.

*Ciabatta, focaccia, or country white bread may be substituted.

ARUGULA-PEAR-BLUE
CHEESE SALAD

FRESH PEAR-AND-GREEN BEAN SALAD

MAKES: 8 servings ▪ HANDS-ON TIME: 15 min. ▪ TOTAL TIME: 1 hour, 15 min.

8   oz. haricots verts (thin green
    beans), trimmed
1   (5-oz.) package gourmet mixed
    salad greens
2   red Bartlett pears, cut into
    thin strips
½   small red onion, sliced
2   cups Sweet-and-Spicy Pecans
4   oz. Gorgonzola cheese, crumbled
Sorghum Vinaigrette

Cook beans in boiling salted water to cover 3 to 4 minutes or until crisp-tender; drain. Plunge beans into ice water to stop cooking process; drain. Toss together salad greens, next 4 ingredients, and beans. Serve with Sorghum Vinaigrette.

Sweet-and-Spicy Pecans

MAKES: 2 cups ▪ HANDS-ON TIME: 10 min. ▪ TOTAL TIME: 1 hour

¼   cup sorghum syrup
2   Tbsp. Demerara sugar
½   tsp. kosher salt
¼   tsp. ground red pepper
2   cups pecan halves
Parchment paper

1. Preheat oven to 350°. Stir together first 4 ingredients. Add pecan halves; stir until coated. Line a jelly-roll pan with parchment paper, and lightly grease paper. Arrange pecans in a single layer in pan.

2. Bake at 350° for 15 minutes or until glaze bubbles slowly and thickens, stirring once after 8 minutes. Transfer pan to a wire rack. Separate pecans into individual pieces; cool completely in pan, about 35 minutes. If cooled pecans are not crisp, bake 5 more minutes.

Sorghum Vinaigrette

MAKES: 2 cups ▪ HANDS-ON TIME: 5 min. ▪ TOTAL TIME: 5 min.

½   cup sorghum syrup
½   cup malt or apple cider vinegar
3   Tbsp. bourbon
2   tsp. grated onion
1   tsp. salt
1   tsp. freshly ground black pepper
½   tsp. hot sauce
1   cup olive oil

Whisk together first 7 ingredients until blended. Add oil in a slow, steady stream, whisking until smooth.

LEMON BROCCOLINI

MAKES: 6 to 8 servings ▪ **HANDS-ON TIME:** 20 min. ▪ **TOTAL TIME:** 20 min.

1   cup (½-inch) French bread
      baguette cubes
2   Tbsp. butter
1   garlic clove, pressed
2   Tbsp. chopped fresh flat-leaf
      parsley
2   tsp. lemon zest
1½ lb. fresh Broccolini
2   Tbsp. fresh lemon juice
1   Tbsp. olive oil

1. Process bread in a food processor 30 seconds to 1 minute or until coarsely crumbled.
2. Melt butter with garlic in a large skillet over medium heat; add breadcrumbs, and cook, stirring constantly, 2 to 3 minutes or until golden brown. Remove from heat, and stir in parsley and lemon zest.
3. Cook Broccolini in boiling salted water to cover 3 to 4 minutes or until crisp-tender; drain well. Toss Broccolini with lemon juice and olive oil. Add salt and pepper to taste. Transfer to a serving platter, and sprinkle with breadcrumb mixture.

ASPARAGUS SAUTÉ

MAKES: 6 servings ▪ **HANDS-ON TIME:** 15 min. ▪ **TOTAL TIME:** 15 min.

2   lb. fresh asparagus
¼   cup butter
1   large red bell pepper, diced
½   tsp. table salt
½   tsp. freshly ground black pepper

1. Cut asparagus into 2-inch pieces, discarding tough ends.
2. Melt butter in a large skillet over medium heat. Add asparagus, bell pepper, and remaining ingredients; sauté 4 to 5 minutes or until crisp-tender. Serve immediately.

PLAN AHEAD
This dish comes together quickly when you prepare the asparagus and chop the red bell pepper the night before.

LEMON BROCCOLINI

BALSAMIC GREEN BEANS

MAKES: 8 to 10 servings ▪ **HANDS-ON TIME:** 30 min. ▪ **TOTAL TIME:** 30 min.

2   lb. fresh haricots verts (thin
       green beans), trimmed*
6   large shallots
Vegetable oil
½   cup balsamic vinegar
1   Tbsp. light brown sugar
3   Tbsp. butter
½   cup lightly salted roasted
       almonds, coarsely chopped
½   cup cooked and crumbled
       bacon (about 5 slices)

1. Cook beans in boiling salted water to cover 3 to 4 minutes or until crisp-tender; drain. Plunge beans into ice water to stop the cooking process; drain.
2. Cut shallots crosswise into thin slices; separate into rings. Pour oil to depth of 1 inch in a heavy saucepan; heat over medium-high heat to 350°. Fry shallots, in batches, 1 to 2 minutes or until crisp. Remove from skillet using a slotted spoon; drain on paper towels.
3. Cook vinegar and sugar in a large skillet over medium-high heat, stirring often, 5 to 6 minutes or until reduced to 3 Tbsp. Stir in butter until blended. Add beans, and sauté 5 minutes or until thoroughly heated; add salt and pepper to taste. Arrange on a serving platter. Top with shallots, almonds, and bacon. Serve immediately.

Regular fresh green beans may be substituted. (You'll need to cook a few minutes longer.)

GREEN BEAN-GOAT CHEESE GRATIN

MAKES: 4 servings ▪ **HANDS-ON TIME:** 20 min. ▪ **TOTAL TIME:** 56 min.

2   white bread slices
1   Tbsp. olive oil
¾   cup (3 oz.) freshly shredded
       Parmesan cheese, divided
⅓   cup finely chopped pecans
1   lb. fresh haricots verts (thin
       green beans), trimmed
2   oz. goat cheese, crumbled
½   cup whipping cream
¼   tsp. kosher salt
¼   tsp. freshly ground black pepper

1. Preheat oven to 400°. Tear bread into large pieces; pulse in a food processor 2 or 3 times or until coarse crumbs form. Drizzle oil over crumbs; add ¼ cup Parmesan cheese. Pulse 5 or 6 times or until coated with oil. Stir in pecans.

2. Cut green beans crosswise into thirds. Cook in boiling water to cover 3 to 4 minutes or until crisp-tender; drain. Plunge into ice water to stop cooking process; drain and pat dry with paper towels.

3. Toss together beans, next 4 ingredients, and remaining ½ cup Parmesan cheese. Firmly pack mixture into 4 (6-oz.) shallow ramekins. Cover each with aluminum foil, and place on a baking sheet.

4. Bake at 400° for 20 minutes. Uncover and sprinkle with crumb mixture. Bake 8 more minutes or until golden. Let stand 5 minutes.

HOLIDAY TRADITION

Host a Christmas dinner and have each guest bring a favorite side dish or special family recipe that reminds them of a Christmas past. Green bean casseroles are a classic in the South. Bread slices, haricots verts, and crumbled goat cheese give this recipe an updated twist.

FRIED CONFETTI CORN

GREEN BEANS WITH
CARAMELIZED SHALLOTS

FRIED CONFETTI CORN

MAKES: 8 servings ▪ **HANDS-ON TIME:** 30 min. ▪ **TOTAL TIME:** 30 min.

8   bacon slices
6   cups fresh sweet corn kernels
      (about 8 ears)
1   cup diced sweet onion
½   cup chopped red bell pepper
½   cup chopped green bell pepper
1   (8-oz.) package cream cheese,
      cubed
½   cup half-and-half
1   tsp. sugar
1   tsp. table salt
1   tsp. freshly ground black pepper

1. Cook bacon in a large skillet over medium-high heat 6 to 8 minutes or until crisp. Remove bacon, and drain on paper towels, reserving 2 Tbsp. drippings in skillet. Coarsely crumble bacon.
2. Sauté corn and next 3 ingredients in hot drippings in skillet over medium-high heat 6 minutes or until tender. Add cream cheese and half-and-half, stirring until cream cheese melts. Stir in sugar and next 2 ingredients. Transfer to a serving dish, and top with bacon.

GREEN BEANS
with Caramelized Shallots

MAKES: 8 servings ▪ **HANDS-ON TIME:** 20 min. ▪ **TOTAL TIME:** 30 min.

2   lb. haricots verts (thin green
      beans), trimmed
3   Tbsp. butter
1   Tbsp. light brown sugar
1   Tbsp. olive oil
1   lb. shallots, halved lengthwise
      and peeled
2   Tbsp. red wine vinegar

1. Cook green beans in boiling salted water to cover 3 to 4 minutes or until crisp-tender; drain. Plunge beans into ice water to stop the cooking process; drain.
2. Melt butter and brown sugar with olive oil in a large skillet over medium-high heat; add shallots, and sauté 2 minutes. Reduce heat to medium-low, add vinegar, and sauté 10 minutes or until shallots are golden brown and tender.
3. Increase heat to medium-high; add green beans, and sauté 5 minutes or until thoroughly heated. Season with salt and freshly ground pepper to taste.

BALSAMIC-ROASTED CARROTS AND PARSNIPS

MAKES: 8 to 10 servings ▪ **HANDS-ON TIME:** 20 min. ▪ **TOTAL TIME:** 1 hour

1   (4-oz.) package feta cheese, crumbled
½   cup chopped sweetened dried cherries
¼   cup chopped fresh flat-leaf parsley
1   tsp. lemon zest
½   tsp. dried crushed red pepper
4   Tbsp. olive oil, divided
1½   lb. carrots
1½   lb. parsnips
2   Tbsp. light brown sugar
1   Tbsp. balsamic vinegar

1. Preheat oven to 400°. Toss together first 5 ingredients and 1 Tbsp. olive oil in a small bowl.
2. Cut carrots and parsnips lengthwise into long, thin strips.
3. Whisk together brown sugar, balsamic vinegar, and remaining 3 Tbsp. olive oil in a large bowl. Toss with carrots and parsnips, and place on a lightly greased 15- x 10-inch jelly-roll pan. Add salt and pepper to taste.
4. Bake at 400° for 40 to 45 minutes or until vegetables are tender and browned, stirring every 15 minutes. Transfer to a serving platter, and gently toss with feta cheese mixture.

CRANBERRY-ROASTED
WINTER VEGETABLES

CRANBERRY-ROASTED WINTER VEGETABLES

MAKES: 8 servings ▪ HANDS-ON TIME: 30 min. ▪ TOTAL TIME: 1 hour, 5 min.

4   large carrots (about 1 1/2 lb.),
    halved lengthwise and cut into
    1-inch pieces
3   large turnips (about 2 lb.),
    peeled and cut into 1-inch pieces*
1   lb. Brussels sprouts, halved
    (quartered, if large)
1   Tbsp. minced fresh rosemary
2   Tbsp. olive oil
3/4   tsp. table salt
1/4   tsp. freshly ground black pepper
1   cup fresh or thawed frozen
    cranberries
4   tsp. molasses

1. Preheat oven to 400°. Lightly grease 2 large jelly-roll pans; place carrots and turnips in one pan and Brussels sprouts in second pan. Divide rosemary and next 3 ingredients between carrot mixture and Brussels sprouts; toss each to coat.

2. Bake both pans at 400° at same time. Bake carrot mixture 30 minutes, stirring once; add cranberries, and bake 5 more minutes or until carrots and turnips are tender and browned and cranberries begin to soften. Bake Brussels sprouts 15 to 20 minutes or until tender and browned, stirring once.

3. Remove vegetables from oven, and combine in a large serving bowl. Drizzle with molasses, and toss to coat.

2 lb. parsnips may be substituted.

ORANGE-GLAZED SWEET POTATOES

MAKES: 8 servings ▪ HANDS-ON TIME: 15 min. ▪ TOTAL TIME: 1 hour, 5 min.

6   medium-size sweet potatoes
    (about 4 lb.)
1/4   cup firmly packed dark
    brown sugar
1/2   tsp. orange zest
1   cup fresh orange juice
2   Tbsp. butter, melted
1/4   tsp. kosher salt
1/4   tsp. ground cinnamon

1. Preheat oven to 325°. Peel potatoes, and cut into 1-inch-thick slices; arrange in a single layer in 2 lightly greased 13- x 9-inch baking dishes.

2. Stir together brown sugar and next 5 ingredients; pour over potatoes. Cover with aluminum foil.

3. Bake at 325° for 45 minutes or until fork-tender. Uncover and bake 5 more minutes or until glaze becomes syrupy.

Make Ahead: Cover and chill cooked potatoes up to 1 day. To reheat, let stand at room temperature 1 hour. Bake, uncovered, at 350° for 20 minutes.

SWEET POTATO-CARROT CASSEROLE

MAKES: 8 to 10 servings ▪ **HANDS-ON TIME:** 30 min. ▪ **TOTAL TIME:** 3 hours

6   large sweet potatoes (about 5 lb.)
1½ lb. carrots, sliced
¼   cup butter
1   cup sour cream
2   Tbsp. sugar
1   tsp. lemon zest
½   tsp. ground nutmeg
½   tsp. table salt
½   tsp. freshly ground black pepper
1½ cups miniature marshmallows
1   cup Sugar-and-Spice Pecans

1. Preheat oven to 400°. Bake sweet potatoes on an aluminum foil-lined 15- x 10-inch jelly-roll pan 1 hour or until tender. Reduce oven temperature to 350°. Cool potatoes 30 minutes.

2. Meanwhile, cook carrots in boiling water to cover 20 to 25 minutes or until very tender; drain.

3. Process carrots and butter in a food processor until smooth, stopping to scrape down sides as needed. Transfer carrot mixture to a large bowl.

4. Peel and cube sweet potatoes. Process, in batches, in food processor until smooth, stopping to scrape down sides as needed. Add sweet potatoes to carrot mixture. Stir in sour cream and next 5 ingredients, stirring until blended. Spoon mixture into a lightly greased 13- x 9-inch baking dish.

5. Bake at 350° for 30 minutes or until thoroughly heated. Remove from oven. Sprinkle with marshmallows. Bake 10 more minutes or until marshmallows are golden brown. Remove from oven, and sprinkle with Sugar-and-Spice Pecans.

Make Ahead: Prepare recipe as directed through Step 4; cover and chill up to 24 hours. Remove from refrigerator, and let stand 30 minutes. Proceed with recipe as directed in Step 5.

Sugar-and-Spice Pecans

MAKES: 4 cups ▪ **HANDS-ON TIME:** 15 min. ▪ **TOTAL TIME:** 1 hour, 10 min.

1   large egg white
4   cups pecan halves and pieces
½   cup sugar
1   Tbsp. orange zest
1   tsp. ground cinnamon
1   tsp. ground ginger

1. Preheat oven to 350°. Whisk egg white in a large bowl until foamy. Add pecans, and stir until evenly coated.

2. Stir together sugar and next 3 ingredients in a small bowl until blended. Sprinkle sugar mixture over pecans; stir gently until pecans are evenly coated. Spread pecans in a single layer in a lightly greased aluminum foil-lined 15- x 10-inch jelly-roll pan.

3. Bake at 350° for 24 to 26 minutes or until pecans are toasted and dry, stirring once after 10 minutes. Remove from oven, and cool completely (about 30 minutes).

Make Ahead: Prepare pecans as directed. Store in a zip-top plastic freezer bag at room temperature up to 3 days, or freeze up to 3 weeks.

CREAMY SPINACH
MASHED POTATO BAKE

CARAMELIZED ONION
MASHED POTATO BAKE

SMOKY SWEET POTATO
MASHED POTATO BAKE

BACON-AND-
BLUE CHEESE
MASHED POTATO
BAKE

TASTY TEX-MEX
MASHED POTATO
BAKE

BUTTERMILK MASHED POTATOES

MAKES: 6 to 8 servings ▪ **HANDS-ON TIME:** 25 min. ▪ **TOTAL TIME:** 50 min.

4   lb. baking potatoes, peeled
     and cut into 2-inch pieces
3   tsp. table salt, divided
¾   cup warm buttermilk
½   cup warm milk
¼   cup butter, melted
½   tsp. freshly ground black pepper

1. Bring potatoes, 2 tsp. salt, and water to cover to a boil in a large Dutch oven over medium-high heat; boil 20 minutes or until tender. Drain. Reduce heat to low. Return potatoes to Dutch oven, and cook, stirring occasionally, 3 to 5 minutes or until potatoes are dry.

2. Mash potatoes with a potato masher to desired consistency. Stir in buttermilk, milk, butter, black pepper, and remaining 1 tsp. salt, stirring just until blended.

Try these twists!

Prepare Buttermilk Mashed Potatoes as directed, increasing buttermilk to 1¼ cups. Stir in one of the tasty combos below, and spoon the mixture into a lightly greased 2½-qt. baking dish or 8 (10-oz.) ramekins. Bake at 350° for 35 minutes.

Smoky Sweet Potato Mashed Potato Bake: 1 cup mashed baked sweet potatoes and 1½ Tbsp. chopped canned chipotle peppers in adobo sauce

Creamy Spinach Mashed Potato Bake: 1 (5-oz.) package fresh baby spinach, wilted; 1 (5½-oz.) package buttery garlic-and-herb spreadable cheese; and ¼ cup chopped toasted pecans

Caramelized Onion Mashed Potato Bake: 1¼ cups freshly grated Gruyère cheese, 1 cup chopped caramelized onions, and 2 Tbsp. chopped fresh parsley

Bacon-and-Blue Cheese Mashed Potato Bake: 1 (4-oz.) wedge blue cheese, crumbled, and 8 cooked and crumbled bacon slices

Tasty Tex-Mex Mashed Potato Bake: 1 (4.5-oz.) can chopped green chiles, 1¼ cups (5 oz.) shredded pepper Jack cheese, and ½ cup finely chopped cooked chorizo sausage

FENNEL-AND-POTATO GRATIN

MAKES: 8 servings ▪ **HANDS-ON TIME:** 30 min. ▪ **TOTAL TIME:** 1 hour, 22 min.

3 Tbsp. butter
1 shallot, sliced
1 garlic clove, minced
2 Tbsp. all-purpose flour
1¼ cups half-and-half
½ (10-oz.) block sharp white
Cheddar cheese, shredded
½ tsp. table salt
¼ tsp. freshly ground black pepper
⅛ tsp. ground nutmeg
2 large baking potatoes
(about 2 lb.), peeled and thinly
sliced
1 small fennel bulb, thinly sliced
Garnish: fresh rosemary sprigs

1. Preheat oven to 400°. Melt butter in a heavy saucepan over medium heat. Add shallot, and sauté 2 to 3 minutes or until tender. Add garlic, and sauté 1 minute.

2. Whisk in flour; cook, whisking constantly, 1 minute. Gradually whisk in half-and-half, and cook, whisking constantly, 3 to 4 minutes or until thickened and bubbly. Remove from heat. Whisk in cheese until melted and smooth. Stir in salt and next 2 ingredients.

3. Layer potato and fennel slices alternately in a lightly greased, broiler-safe 2-qt. baking dish. Spread cheese sauce over layers. Cover with aluminum foil.

4. Bake at 400° for 50 minutes or until potatoes are tender. Remove from oven. Increase oven temperature to broil with oven rack 5 inches from heat. Uncover and broil 2 to 4 minutes or until golden brown.

WRAP IT UP

Potted rosemary, the sign of love and friendship, makes the perfect Christmas gift. Wrap the pot in burlap, tie with ribbon, and attach a favorite holiday recipe, such as this one, that uses the fragrant herb.

BUTTERNUT SQUASH GRATIN

MAKES: 8 servings ▪ **HANDS-ON TIME:** 45 min. ▪ **TOTAL TIME:** 3 hours, 30 min.

1 (3-lb.) butternut squash
1 (3-lb.) spaghetti squash
2 Tbsp. butter, melted
1 cup firmly packed light brown
    sugar, divided
½ tsp. ground cinnamon
¼ tsp. ground nutmeg
3 cups whipping cream
5 large Yukon gold potatoes
    (about 2½ lb.)
1 tsp. table salt
1 tsp. freshly ground black pepper
4 cups (16 oz.) freshly shredded
    fontina cheese*
Garnish: fresh rosemary sprigs

*Gouda cheese may be substituted.

Tip: To help prevent the potatoes from turning brown (oxidizing), slice them as you use them in each layer, rather than all at once.

1. Preheat oven to 450°. Cut butternut and spaghetti squash in half lengthwise; remove and discard seeds. Place squash, cut sides up, in a lightly greased 17- x 12-inch jelly-roll pan. Drizzle with butter, and sprinkle with ½ cup brown sugar. Bake at 450° for 40 minutes or until tender. Cool 20 minutes.

2. Using a fork, scrape inside of spaghetti squash to remove spaghetti-like strands, and place in a large bowl. Scoop pulp from butternut squash; coarsely chop pulp, and toss with spaghetti squash.

3. Stir together cinnamon, nutmeg, and remaining ½ cup brown sugar.

4. Cook cream in a heavy nonaluminum saucepan over medium heat, stirring often, 5 minutes or just until it begins to steam (do not boil); remove from heat.

5. Using a mandoline or sharp knife, cut potatoes into ⅛-inch-thick slices.

6. Arrange one-fourth of potato slices in a thin layer on bottom of a greased 13- x 9-inch baking dish. Spoon one-third of squash mixture over potatoes (squash layer should be about ¼ inch thick); sprinkle with ¼ tsp. salt, ¼ tsp. black pepper, 1 cup fontina cheese, and ¾ cup hot cream. Repeat layers twice, sprinkling one-third of sugar mixture over each of second and third squash layers. (Do not sprinkle sugar mixture over first squash layer.) Top with remaining potato slices, ¼ tsp. salt, and ¼ tsp. black pepper. Gently press layers down with back of a spoon. Sprinkle top with remaining 1 cup cheese and ¾ cup hot cream; sprinkle with remaining brown sugar mixture. Place baking dish on an aluminum foil-lined baking sheet.

7. Bake, covered with foil, at 450° for 1 hour; uncover and bake 25 more minutes or until golden brown and potatoes are tender. Cool on a wire rack 20 minutes before serving.

SQUASH CASSEROLE

MAKES: 8 to 10 servings ▪ **HANDS-ON TIME:** 40 min. ▪ **TOTAL TIME:** 1 hour, 15 min.

4　lb. yellow squash, sliced
1　large sweet onion, finely chopped
1　cup (4 oz.) freshly shredded
　　　Cheddar cheese
2　large eggs, lightly beaten
1　cup mayonnaise
2　Tbsp. chopped fresh basil
1　tsp. garlic salt
1　tsp. freshly ground black pepper
2　cups soft, fresh breadcrumbs,
　　　divided
1¼　cups (5 oz.) freshly shredded
　　　Parmesan cheese, divided
2　Tbsp. butter, melted
½　cup crushed French fried onions

1. Preheat oven to 350°. Cook squash and sweet onion in boiling water to cover in a Dutch oven 8 minutes or just until vegetables are tender; drain squash mixture well.

2. Combine squash mixture, freshly shredded Cheddar cheese, next 5 ingredients, 1 cup breadcrumbs, and ¾ cup Parmesan cheese. Spoon into a lightly greased 13- x 9-inch baking dish.

3. Stir together melted butter, French fried onions, and remaining 1 cup breadcrumbs and ½ cup Parmesan cheese. Sprinkle over squash mixture.

4. Bake at 350° for 35 to 40 minutes or until set, shielding with aluminum foil after 20 to 25 minutes to prevent excessive browning, if necessary. Let stand 10 minutes before serving.

Fresh squash and basil, a mix of Parmesan and Cheddar cheeses, and a crunchy breadcrumb topping all make this squash casserole divine.

FOUR-CHEESE MACARONI

MAKES: 8 servings ▪ **HANDS-ON TIME:** 40 min. ▪ **TOTAL TIME:** 1 hour, 15 min.

12   oz. cavatappi pasta
½   cup butter
½   cup all-purpose flour
½   tsp. ground red pepper
3   cups milk
2   cups (8 oz.) freshly shredded
     white Cheddar cheese
1   cup (4 oz.) freshly shredded
     Monterey Jack cheese
1   cup (4 oz.) freshly shredded
     fontina cheese
1   cup (4 oz.) freshly shredded
     Asiago cheese
1½   cups soft, fresh breadcrumbs
½   cup chopped cooked bacon
½   cup chopped pecans
2   Tbsp. butter, melted

1. Preheat oven to 350°. Prepare pasta according to package directions.

2. Meanwhile, melt ½ cup butter in a Dutch oven over low heat; whisk in flour and ground red pepper until smooth. Cook, whisking constantly, 1 minute. Gradually whisk in milk; cook over medium heat, whisking constantly, 6 to 7 minutes or until milk mixture is thickened and bubbly. Remove from heat.

3. Toss together Cheddar cheese and next 3 ingredients in a medium bowl; reserve 1½ cups cheese mixture. Add remaining cheese mixture and hot cooked pasta to sauce, tossing to coat. Spoon into a lightly greased 13- x 9-inch baking dish. Top with reserved 1½ cups cheese mixture.

4. Toss together breadcrumbs and next 3 ingredients; sprinkle over cheese mixture.

5. Bake at 350° for 35 to 40 minutes or until bubbly and golden brown.

HOLIDAY TRADITION

Hosting families with children can be a fun way to celebrate the season, but cooking separate dishes for adults and kids can be tiring. Serve a side such as this macaroni and cheese that the entire party will enjoy.

WILD RICE
with Bacon and Fennel

MAKES: 8 servings ▪ **HANDS-ON TIME:** 40 min. ▪ **TOTAL TIME:** 1 hour, 5 min.

1⅓ cups uncooked wild rice
4 bacon slices
1 large fennel bulb, thinly sliced
1 large onion, cut into thin wedges
2 garlic cloves, minced
½ cup reduced-sodium fat-free
   chicken broth
⅓ cup golden raisins
¼ tsp. table salt
⅛ tsp. freshly ground black pepper
¼ cup chopped fresh fennel
   fronds or flat-leaf parsley
1 Tbsp. white wine vinegar
½ cup chopped toasted walnuts

1. Cook wild rice according to package directions; drain.
2. Meanwhile, cook bacon in a large nonstick skillet over medium-high heat 7 to 8 minutes or until crisp; remove bacon, and drain on paper towels, reserving 1 Tbsp. drippings in skillet. Chop bacon.
3. Sauté fennel bulb and onion in hot drippings over medium-high heat 5 minutes or until softened. Add garlic; sauté 1 minute. Add broth and next 3 ingredients; bring to a boil. Reduce heat to medium-low; cover and simmer 8 minutes or until vegetables are tender. Stir in rice and bacon; cook, stirring often, 3 minutes.
4. Transfer to a large serving bowl. Stir in fennel fronds and vinegar. Stir in walnuts just before serving.

Tip: *For the best texture, use wild rice, not a blend.*

WILD RICE
with Mushrooms

MAKES: 8 to 10 servings ▪ **HANDS-ON TIME:** 30 min. ▪ **TOTAL TIME:** 30 min.

2 (6-oz.) packages long-grain and
   wild rice mix
3 Tbsp. butter
1 large sweet onion, diced
12 oz. assorted fresh mushrooms,
   trimmed and sliced
¼ tsp. table salt
½ cup Marsala
½ cup chopped fresh flat-leaf
   parsley

1. Cook rice mix according to package directions.
2. Meanwhile, melt butter in a large skillet over medium-high heat; add onion, and sauté 7 minutes or until golden. Add mushrooms and salt; sauté 4 to 5 minutes or until mushrooms are tender. Add Marsala, and sauté 3 minutes or until liquid is absorbed. Stir mushroom mixture and parsley into prepared rice.

WILD RICE WITH BACON
AND FENNEL

CREOLE CORNBREAD DRESSING

MAKES: 14 to 16 servings ▪ **HANDS-ON TIME:** 55 min. ▪ **TOTAL TIME:** 2 hours, 55 min.

1　(12-oz.) package andouille
　　sausage, chopped
8　green onions, thinly sliced
3　large celery ribs, diced
1　large sweet onion, diced
1　medium-size green bell pepper,
　　diced
Cornbread Crumbles
½　cup butter
1　(8-oz.) package fresh
　　mushrooms, diced
1　cup dry sherry
½　cup chopped fresh parsley
2　cups chopped toasted pecans
2　Tbsp. Creole seasoning
2　(14-oz.) cans reduced-sodium
　　fat-free chicken broth
2　large eggs

1. Preheat oven to 350°. Sauté andouille sausage in a large skillet over medium-high heat 3 to 4 minutes or until lightly browned. Add green onions and next 3 ingredients, and sauté 5 minutes or until vegetables are tender. Transfer mixture to a large bowl; stir in Cornbread Crumbles.
2. Melt butter in skillet over medium-high heat; add mushrooms, and sauté 3 minutes. Add sherry, and cook, stirring often, 5 to 6 minutes or until liquid is reduced by half; stir in parsley. Stir mushroom mixture, toasted pecans, and Creole seasoning into cornbread mixture.
3. Whisk together chicken broth and eggs; add to cornbread mixture, stirring gently just until moistened. Divide mixture between 1 lightly greased 13- x 9-inch baking dish and 1 lightly greased 8-inch square baking dish.
4. Bake at 350° for 40 to 45 minutes or until golden brown.

Cornbread Crumbles

MAKES: 1 dressing recipe ▪ **HANDS-ON TIME:** 10 min. ▪ **TOTAL TIME:** 1 hour, 10 min.

3　cups self-rising white
　　cornmeal mix
1　cup all-purpose flour
2　Tbsp. sugar
3　cups buttermilk
3　large eggs, lightly beaten
½　cup butter, melted

Preheat oven to 425°. Stir together first 3 ingredients in a large bowl; whisk in buttermilk, eggs, and butter. Pour batter into a lightly greased 13- x 9-inch pan. Bake at 425° for 30 minutes or until golden brown. Remove from oven, invert onto a wire rack, and cool completely (about 30 minutes); crumble cornbread.

FESTIVE MAIN DISHES

Gather around the table to celebrate this year's blessings with one of these entrées. Make our creamy chicken casserole, glazed ham, or grilled turkey the star of your holiday meal.

PANCETTA-AND-FIG PASTA

Bucatini is a hearty, hollow, spaghetti-like pasta. You can substitute linguine or fettuccine, if you prefer.

MAKES: 6 servings ▪ **HANDS-ON TIME:** 25 min. ▪ **TOTAL TIME:** 35 min.

1　(16-oz.) package bucatini pasta
5　oz. thinly sliced pancetta, chopped (about 1 cup)
2　shallots, minced
1　garlic clove, minced
¾　cup heavy cream
½　cup freshly grated Parmesan cheese
12　fresh figs, quartered
⅓　cup torn basil leaves

1. Cook pasta in boiling salted water according to package directions; drain, reserving 1 cup hot pasta water.

2. Sauté pancetta, shallots, and garlic in a large skillet over medium heat 6 to 7 minutes or until pancetta is golden and shallots are tender. Add cream, cheese, and hot cooked pasta; cook, stirring constantly, 2 to 3 minutes or until cheese melts. Stir in ¾ to 1 cup reserved pasta water until creamy. Add salt and pepper to taste. Transfer to a serving dish. Sprinkle with figs and basil. Serve immediately.

BUTTERNUT SQUASH RAVIOLI WITH MUSHROOMS

MAKES: 8 servings ▪ **HANDS-ON TIME:** 25 min. ▪ **TOTAL TIME:** 25 min.

2　(8-oz.) packages refrigerated butternut squash-filled ravioli
6　Tbsp. butter, divided
1　(8-oz.) package sliced baby portobello mushrooms
4　garlic cloves, thinly sliced
3　Tbsp. sliced fresh shallots
2　Tbsp. chopped fresh flat-leaf parsley
1　Tbsp. thinly sliced fresh sage
1　tsp. kosher salt
¼　tsp. black pepper
Toppings: freshly shaved Parmesan cheese, black pepper, chopped fresh parsley

1. Prepare butternut squash-filled ravioli according to package directions. Keep warm.

2. Melt 2 Tbsp. butter in a large skillet over medium heat. Add mushrooms; sauté 3 to 5 minutes or until lightly browned. Add garlic and shallots; sauté 2 minutes or until tender. Remove from skillet. Wipe skillet clean.

3. Melt remaining 4 Tbsp. butter in skillet over medium heat; cook 2 to 3 minutes or until lightly browned. Stir in parsley, sage, and mushroom mixture. Add hot cooked ravioli, and toss gently. Stir in salt and black pepper. Serve immediately with desired toppings.

Note: We tested with Whole Foods Market 365 Everyday Value Butternut Squash Ravioli.

ROQUEFORT NOODLES

Don't skimp on the quality of the blue cheese in this recipe.

MAKES: 6 to 8 servings ▪ **HANDS-ON TIME:** 20 min. ▪ **TOTAL TIME:** 20 min.

1   (12-oz.) package wide egg
     noodles
1   Tbsp. jarred chicken soup base
½   tsp. olive oil
½   cup butter
6   to 8 green onions, sliced
4   to 6 oz. Roquefort, crumbled
1   (8-oz.) container sour cream

1. Cook egg noodles according to package directions, adding chicken soup base and oil to water.

2. Meanwhile, melt butter in a large heavy skillet over medium heat. Add onions, and sauté 5 to 7 minutes or until tender. Reduce heat to medium-low, and stir in Roquefort cheese, stirring constantly, until cheese is melted. Remove from heat, and stir in sour cream until blended and smooth.

3. Toss together Roquefort cheese sauce and hot cooked egg noodles. Add pepper to taste.

Note: *We tested with Superior Touch Better Than Bouillon Chicken Base.*

HOLIDAY TRADITION

Enjoy more time with the family and less time in the kitchen with this quick 20-minute dish. End the evening around the tree with store-bought cookies and hot cocoa.

CARAMELIZED MAPLE- AND-GARLIC- GLAZED SALMON

MAKES: 8 servings ▪ **HANDS-ON TIME:** 20 min. ▪ **TOTAL TIME:** 20 min.

8 (2-inch-thick) salmon fillets (about 2½ lb.)
¾ tsp. table salt
¾ tsp. garlic powder
2 Tbsp. butter
⅓ cup maple syrup, divided
1 Tbsp. chopped fresh chives

1. Preheat broiler with oven rack 5½ inches from heat. Sprinkle salmon with salt and garlic powder.

2. Melt butter in a large skillet over medium heat. Add salmon, skin side up; cook 2 minutes. Place salmon, skin side down, on a lightly greased rack in a broiler pan; brush with half of syrup.

3. Broil salmon 5 to 7 minutes or until fish reaches desired degree of doneness and syrup begins to caramelize. Brush with remaining syrup; sprinkle with chives.

Maple syrup isn't just for pancakes. When brushed on salmon and broiled, maple syrup delivers a succulent flavor in this delicious main dish.

CREAMY CHICKEN-AND-WILD RICE CASSEROLE

MAKES: 10 to 12 servings ▪ **HANDS-ON TIME:** 30 min. ▪ **TOTAL TIME:** 1 hour, 10 min.

2 (6.2-oz.) boxes fast-cooking long-grain and wild rice mix
¼ cup butter
4 celery ribs, chopped
2 medium onions, chopped
5 cups chopped cooked chicken
2 (10¾-oz.) cans cream of mushroom soup
2 (8-oz.) cans chopped water chestnuts, drained
1 (8-oz.) container sour cream
1 cup milk
½ tsp. table salt
½ tsp. black pepper
4 cups (16 oz.) shredded Cheddar cheese, divided
2 cups soft fresh breadcrumbs
1 (2.25-oz.) package sliced almonds, toasted

1. Prepare rice mixes according to package directions.
2. Meanwhile, melt butter in a large skillet over medium heat; add celery and onions. Sauté 10 minutes or until tender.
3. Preheat oven to 350°. Stir in chicken, next 6 ingredients, rice, and 3 cups cheese. Spoon mixture into a lightly greased 15- x 10-inch baking dish or 2 (11- x 7-inch) baking dishes. Top casserole with breadcrumbs.
4. Bake, uncovered, at 350° for 35 minutes. Sprinkle with remaining 1 cup cheese; top with toasted almonds. Bake 5 more minutes.

Make Ahead: *Prepare recipe as directed through Step 3, excluding the breadcrumbs. Cover with aluminum foil, and freeze up to 1 month. Remove from freezer, and let stand at room temperature 1 hour. Top with breadcrumbs and bake, covered, at 350° for 30 minutes. Uncover casserole, and bake 1 hour and 15 more minutes. Sprinkle with 1 cup (4 oz.) shredded Cheddar cheese, and top with toasted almonds; bake 5 more minutes.*

Try these twists!

Prepare Creamy Chicken-and-Wild Rice Casserole as directed, making the following substitutions.

Shrimp-and-Wild Rice Casserole: Substitute 2 lb. peeled and deveined medium-size raw shrimp for chicken, 2 cups (8 oz.) shredded Monterey Jack cheese and 2 cups grated Parmesan cheese for Cheddar cheese, and 1 cup dry white wine for milk.

Cajun Chicken-and-Wild Rice Casserole: Omit salt and pepper. Reduce chicken to 2½ cups. Prepare as directed, sautéing 1 lb. andouille sausage, chopped, and 1 green bell pepper, diced, with celery in Step 3. Stir 1 (15-oz.) can black-eyed peas, drained, and 1 tsp. Cajun seasoning into rice mixture. Proceed as directed.

SKILLET CHICKEN POT PIE

MAKES: 6 to 8 servings ▪ **HANDS-ON TIME:** 30 min. ▪ **TOTAL TIME:** 1 hour, 30 min.

CHICKEN PIE FILLING

- ⅓ cup butter
- ⅓ cup all-purpose flour
- 1½ cups chicken broth
- 1½ cups milk
- 1½ tsp. Creole seasoning
- 2 Tbsp. butter
- 1 large sweet onion, diced
- 1 (8-oz.) package sliced fresh mushrooms
- 4 cups shredded cooked chicken
- 2 cups frozen cubed hash browns
- 1 cup matchstick carrots
- 1 cup frozen small sweet peas
- ⅓ cup chopped fresh parsley

PASTRY CRUST

- 1 (14.1-oz.) package refrigerated piecrusts
- 1 large egg white

1. Prepare Chicken Pie Filling: Preheat oven to 350°. Melt ⅓ cup butter in a large saucepan over medium heat; add all-purpose flour, and cook, whisking constantly, 1 minute. Gradually add chicken broth and milk, and cook, whisking constantly, 6 to 7 minutes or until thickened and bubbly. Remove from heat, and stir in Creole seasoning.

2. Melt 2 Tbsp. butter in a large Dutch oven over medium-high heat; add onion and mushrooms, and sauté 10 minutes or until tender. Stir in chicken, next 4 ingredients, and sauce.

3. Prepare Pastry Crust: Place 1 piecrust in a lightly greased 10-inch cast-iron skillet. Spoon chicken mixture over piecrust, and top with remaining piecrust.

4. Whisk egg white until foamy; brush top of piecrust with egg white. Cut 4 to 5 slits in top of pie for steam to escape.

5. Bake at 350° for 1 hour to 1 hour and 5 minutes or until golden brown and bubbly.

ROASTED CHICKEN
with Sweet Potatoes and Apples

MAKES: 8 servings ▪ **HANDS-ON TIME:** 40 min. ▪ **TOTAL TIME:** 2 hours, 20 min.

1   lemon
½   cup butter, softened
2   garlic cloves, minced
1   tsp. kosher salt, divided
1   tsp. freshly ground black
    pepper, divided
1   (5- to 6-lb.) whole chicken
3   fresh thyme sprigs
Kitchen string
1   large sweet potato (about 1 lb.)
2   large Granny Smith apples
    (about 1 lb.)
4   Tbsp. firmly packed dark
    brown sugar
¼   cup butter, melted
Garnishes: lemon slices, fresh
    thyme sprigs

1. Preheat oven to 425°. Grate zest from lemon to equal 2 tsp.; reserve lemon. Combine zest, softened butter, garlic, and ½ tsp. each salt and black pepper. If applicable, remove neck and giblets from chicken, and reserve for another use. Rinse chicken, and pat dry. Loosen and lift skin from chicken breast with fingers (do not totally detach skin); spread half of butter mixture underneath skin, and place thyme sprigs under skin. Carefully replace skin.

2. Cut reserved lemon in half. Squeeze lemon juice into cavity of chicken, and place lemon halves in cavity. Tie ends of legs together with string; tuck wingtips under. Rub remaining butter mixture over chicken, and sprinkle with remaining ½ tsp. each salt and black pepper. Place chicken, breast side up, on a lightly greased rack in a lightly greased large, shallow roasting pan.

3. Bake chicken at 425° for 30 minutes.

4. Meanwhile, peel sweet potato and apples. Cut potato in half lengthwise, and cut into ¼-inch-thick half-moon slices. Cut apples in half vertically through stem and bottom ends, and cut into ¼-inch-thick wedges. Arrange half of sweet potatoes in bottom of a 9-inch oval gratin dish. Sprinkle with 1 Tbsp. brown sugar. Arrange apple wedges in a single layer over sweet potatoes; sprinke with 1 Tbsp. brown sugar. Top with remaining sweet potatoes, and sprinkle with remaining 2 Tbsp. brown sugar; drizzle with ¼ cup melted butter. Add salt and pepper to taste.

5. Reduce oven temperature to 350°. Bake chicken 15 more minutes. Add potato mixture to oven, and bake chicken and potato mixture at same time for 35 minutes. Uncover potato mixture, and bake 40 more minutes or until a meat thermometer inserted into thickest portion of chicken thigh registers 165° and potatoes and apples are tender and lightly browned.

BAKED CHICKEN ROULADE

MAKES: 4 servings ▪ **HANDS-ON TIME:** 30 min. ▪ **TOTAL TIME:** 45 min.

4   *skinned and boned chicken breasts (about 1½ lb.)*
½   *tsp. black pepper*
¼   *tsp. table salt*
1   *(5-oz.) package fresh baby spinach*
4   *garlic cloves, minced and divided*
2   *tsp. olive oil*
12 *fresh thin asparagus spears (about 1 lb.)*
Wooden picks
5   *Tbsp. butter, divided*
2   *Tbsp. olive oil*
1   *Tbsp. all-purpose flour*
2   *Tbsp. dry white wine*
¾   *cup chicken broth*
1   *tsp. fresh lemon juice*
2   *Tbsp. chopped fresh flat-leaf parsley*
2   *Tbsp. drained capers*

1. Preheat oven to 425°. Place chicken between 2 sheets of heavy-duty plastic wrap, and flatten to ¼-inch thickness using flat side of a meat mallet or rolling pin. Sprinkle chicken with black pepper and salt.

2. Sauté spinach and 2 minced garlic cloves in 2 tsp. hot oil in a large ovenproof skillet over medium heat 1 minute or until spinach begins to wilt. Transfer spinach mixture to a plate. Wipe skillet clean.

3. Spoon spinach mixture over each breast, leaving a ½-inch border around edges. Top with asparagus, and roll up, starting at 1 short side. Tuck in ends of chicken, and secure with wooden picks.

4. Melt 3 Tbsp. butter with 2 Tbsp. oil in skillet over medium-high heat; add chicken. Cook 6 to 8 minutes, turning to brown on all sides. Transfer skillet to oven, and bake at 425° for 15 minutes. Transfer to a serving plate, and cover loosely with aluminum foil to keep warm.

5. Melt remaining 2 Tbsp. butter in skillet over medium-high heat; add remaining garlic. Sauté 1 to 2 minutes or until tender and fragrant. Whisk in flour; cook 1 minute. Add white wine; cook, stirring constantly, 1 minute. Whisk in chicken broth and lemon juice; cook 2 minutes or until thickened. Stir in parsley and capers; spoon sauce over chicken, and serve immediately.

FIG-AND-BALSAMIC-GLAZED QUAIL

Call ahead to be sure your butcher has quail on hand. For a delicious alternative, use cornish hens. (See Fig-and-Balsamic-Glazed Cornish Hens below.)

MAKES: 8 servings ▪ **HANDS-ON TIME:** 20 min. ▪ **TOTAL TIME:** 1 hour, 15 min.

1   (11.5-oz.) jar fig preserves
½   cup dry red wine
3   Tbsp. balsamic vinegar
½   tsp. coarsely ground black
      pepper
2   tsp. country-style Dijon mustard
8   (3.5-oz.) semiboneless quail
Kitchen string
1   tsp. kosher salt
2   Tbsp. dry red wine

1. Preheat oven to 450°. Bring first 5 ingredients to a boil in a small saucepan over medium-high heat; reduce heat to low, and simmer 8 to 10 minutes or until slightly thickened. Reserve half of fig mixture; cover and chill. Let remaining fig mixture stand at room temperature.
2. Tie ends of quail legs together with string.
3. Place quail on an aluminum foil-lined jelly-roll pan or in a shallow roasting pan, and sprinkle with salt.
4. Bake at 450° for 10 minutes. Brush quail generously with room-temperature fig mixture. Reduce oven temperature to 400°. Bake quail 30 more minutes or until leg meat is no longer pink, basting with fig mixture every 10 minutes.
5. Place reserved chilled fig mixture in a small saucepan; stir in dry red wine, and cook over low heat, stirring often, 2 minutes or until thoroughly heated. Serve quail with sauce.

Make Ahead: Prepare recipe as directed through Step 3. Cover and chill up to 8 hours. Let stand at room temperature 15 minutes before proceeding with Steps 4 and 5.

Try this twist!

Fig-and-Balsamic-Glazed Cornish Hens: Substitute 4 (1¼- to 1½-lb.) cornish hens for quail. Prepare Step 1 as directed; omit Step 2. Rinse hens with cold water, and pat dry. Place hens, breast sides down, on a cutting board. Cut hens through backbone using kitchen shears to make 2 halves. Proceed with recipe as directed in Steps 3 through 5, increasing second bake time (at 400°) to 45 minutes. Let stand 10 minutes before serving.

GRILLED TURKEY BREAST

MAKES: 8 servings ▪ HANDS-ON TIME: 20 min. ▪ TOTAL TIME: 9 hours, 35 min., including salsa

⅓ cup kosher salt
⅓ cup sugar
3 bay leaves
2 jalapeño peppers, halved
2 Tbsp. cumin seeds
1 (5- to 6-lb.) boned, skin-on fresh
    turkey breast*
1 Tbsp. table salt
1 Tbsp. cumin seeds
1 Tbsp. paprika
2 tsp. freshly ground black pepper
1 tsp. ground coriander
1 tsp. dried oregano
Parsley-Mint Salsa Verde

1. Stir together kosher salt, next 4 ingredients, and 2 qt. water in a large, deep food-safe container or stockpot until sugar dissolves. Add turkey. Chill 8 hours or overnight, turning once.

2. Coat cold cooking grate of grill with cooking spray, and place on grill. Light 1 side of grill, heating to 350° to 400° (medium-high) heat; leave other side unlit. Remove turkey from brine. Rinse turkey, drain well, and pat dry with paper towels.

3. Stir together table salt and next 5 ingredients. Rub skin of turkey with mixture.

4. Place turkey, skin side down, over lit side of grill, and grill, without grill lid, 4 to 5 minutes or until slightly charred. Transfer to unlit side, skin side up. Grill, covered with grill lid, 30 to 40 more minutes or until a meat thermometer inserted into thickest portion registers 165°. Return turkey, skin side down, to lit side, and grill, covered with grill lid, 4 to 5 more minutes or until skin is crisp.

5. Remove turkey from heat; cover loosely with aluminum foil. Let stand 10 minutes. Serve with salsa verde.

*Frozen turkey breast, thawed, may be substituted.

Parsley-Mint Salsa Verde

MAKES: 1¾ cups ▪ HANDS-ON TIME: 15 min. ▪ TOTAL TIME: 35 min.

⅔ cup extra virgin olive oil
⅓ cup sherry vinegar
¼ cup finely chopped shallots
2 garlic cloves, finely chopped
1 tsp. table salt
½ tsp. freshly ground black pepper
1 cup chopped fresh flat-leaf
    parsley
¾ cup chopped fresh mint

Whisk together first 6 ingredients and 2 Tbsp. water until salt dissolves. Whisk in parsley and mint. Let stand 20 minutes.

TURKEY TENDERLOINS
with Madeira Gravy

MAKES: 12 servings ▪ HANDS-ON TIME: 40 min. ▪ TOTAL TIME: 3 hours, 10 min.

3   *cups dry Madeira or fino sherry*
¾   *cup red wine vinegar*
12   *garlic cloves, crushed*
18   *fresh thyme sprigs*
3   *tsp. kosher salt, divided*
4   *lb. turkey tenderloins*
2   *Tbsp. vegetable oil, divided*
1   *tsp. freshly ground black pepper*
3   *Tbsp. butter*
3   *large shallots, finely chopped*
2   *tsp. sifted all-purpose flour*
Garnish: fresh thyme sprigs

1. Stir together first 4 ingredients and 2 tsp. salt in a 2-qt. measuring cup until salt dissolves. Reserve 1¼ cups. Pour remaining mixture into a zip-top plastic freezer bag. Add tenderloins; press out air, seal, and chill 2 to 4 hours, turning every 30 minutes.

2. Preheat oven to 450°. Remove tenderloins from marinade, discarding marinade. Pat tenderloins dry. Brush with 1 Tbsp. oil, and sprinkle with pepper and remaining 1 tsp. salt.

3. Cook tenderloins, in batches, in remaining 1 Tbsp. hot oil in a large cast-iron skillet over high heat 2 to 3 minutes on each side or until browned. Transfer to a plate; discard oil. Reduce heat to medium. Add butter and shallots to skillet, and cook, stirring constantly, until butter melts. Stir in flour. Cook, stirring often, 3 minutes or until shallots are tender. Whisk in reserved 1¼ cups sherry mixture, and bring to a simmer. Simmer 2 to 3 minutes or until slightly thickened. Remove from heat, and add salt and pepper to taste. Place tenderloins in a 13- x 9-inch baking dish; pour sauce over tenderloins.

4. Bake at 450° for 10 to 12 minutes or until a meat thermometer inserted into thickest portion registers 165°. Transfer tenderloins to a cutting board, reserving gravy in baking dish. Cover loosely with aluminum foil, and let stand 10 minutes. Cut into ½-inch-thick medallions, and serve with gravy.

Make Ahead: *The turkey tenderloins marinate for 2 to 4 hours, making it an easy make-ahead dish. Prepare your side dishes while the tenderloins chill.*

HERB-ROASTED TURKEY

MAKES: 8 servings ▪ **HANDS-ON TIME:** 1 hour ▪ **TOTAL TIME:** 6 hours

1 (14-lb.) whole fresh turkey*
Kitchen string
1 tsp. dried thyme
1 tsp. ground sage
½ tsp. dried tarragon
3 tsp. table salt
1 tsp. freshly ground black pepper
¼ cup butter, softened
2 medium onions, chopped
2 carrots, chopped
2 celery ribs, chopped
1 garlic bulb, halved
1 cup dry white wine
Garnish: fresh sage leaves

1. Remove giblets and neck from turkey, and rinse turkey with cold water. Drain cavity well; pat dry. Tie ends of legs together with string; tuck wingtips under. Place, breast side up, on a lightly greased roasting rack in a large roasting pan. Let stand at room temperature 1 hour.

2. Preheat oven to 400°. Stir together thyme, next 2 ingredients, 1½ tsp. salt, and ½ tsp. black pepper; rub mixture into cavity of turkey. Rub butter over turkey. Sprinkle remaining salt and black pepper over outside of turkey; rub into skin. Arrange onions and next 3 ingredients around base of turkey in roasting pan; add wine and 1 cup water to pan.

3. Place turkey in oven; reduce oven temperature to 325°. Bake at 325° for 3 hours or until a meat thermometer inserted into thickest portion of thigh registers 160°.

4. Remove turkey from oven; increase heat to 425°. Baste turkey with pan juices, and let stand 15 minutes; return to oven. Bake at 425° for 10 to 15 minutes or until golden brown and thermometer registers 165°.

5. Let turkey stand in pan 30 minutes; transfer to a serving platter. Reserve pan drippings for Easy Turkey Gravy, if desired.

Frozen whole turkey, thawed, may be substituted.

Easy Turkey Gravy

MAKES: 6 cups ▪ **HANDS-ON TIME:** 25 min. ▪ **TOTAL TIME:** 25 min.

Reserved pan drippings from
    Herb-Roasted Turkey
Chicken broth (up to 2 ½ cups),
    divided
¼ cup butter
¼ cup all-purpose flour

1. Pour reserved pan drippings through a wire-mesh strainer into a large measuring cup, discarding solids. Add broth to equal 3 cups.

2. Melt butter in a saucepan over medium heat; whisk in flour, and cook, whisking constantly, 10 to 12 minutes or until smooth and light brown. (Mixture should be color of peanut butter.) Gradually whisk in drippings mixture. Bring to a boil, whisking constantly. Reduce heat to medium-low; simmer, stirring occasionally, 5 minutes or until thickened. Add up to ½ cup broth for desired consistency. Add salt and pepper to taste.

APPLE-BOURBON TURKEY AND GRAVY

Apple slices and aromatic vegetables line the roasting pan, creating a colorful rack that adds terrific flavor to both the turkey and pan juices.

MAKES: 8 servings ▪ **HANDS-ON TIME:** 55 min. ▪ **TOTAL TIME:** 16 hours, 40 min.

4   cups apple juice
1   cup bourbon
½   cup firmly packed light brown
       sugar
1   (12- to 15-lb.) whole fresh turkey*
Cheesecloth
Kitchen string
4   celery ribs
4   large carrots
3   small apples, quartered
       or halved
1   large onion, sliced
¼   cup butter
¼   cup all-purpose flour
½   cup chicken broth (optional)

1. Stir together apple juice and next 2 ingredients, stirring until sugar dissolves.

2. Remove giblets and neck from turkey, and rinse turkey with cold water. Drain cavity well; pat dry. Place turkey in a large roasting pan. Dip cheesecloth in apple juice mixture; wring dry. Cover turkey with cheesecloth; pour apple juice mixture over cheesecloth, coating completely. Cover and chill 12 to 24 hours, basting occasionally with marinade.

3. Preheat oven to 325°. Remove turkey from pan, discarding cheesecloth and reserving 3 cups marinade. Sprinkle cavity with salt; rub into cavity. Add salt and freshly ground pepper on skin; rub into skin. Tie ends of legs together with string; tuck wingtips under.

4. Arrange celery and next 3 ingredients in a single layer in bottom of roasting pan. Place turkey, breast side up, on celery mixture; pour reserved marinade over turkey in pan.

5. Bake at 325° for 3 hours and 15 minutes to 4 hours or until a meat thermometer inserted into thickest portion of thigh registers 165°, basting every 30 minutes with pan juices and shielding with aluminum foil after 2 hours and 30 minutes to prevent excessive browning, if necessary. Remove from oven, and let stand 30 minutes.

6. Transfer turkey to a serving platter, reserving 2½ cups pan drippings. Pour reserved drippings through a fine wire-mesh strainer into a large measuring cup; discard solids.

7. Melt butter in a saucepan over medium heat; whisk in flour, and cook, whisking constantly, 1 to 2 minutes or until smooth. Gradually add drippings to pan, and bring to a boil. Reduce heat to medium, and simmer, stirring occasionally, 5 minutes or until gravy thickens. Add up to ½ cup chicken broth for desired consistency. Add salt and freshly ground black pepper to taste. Serve turkey with warm gravy.

*Frozen whole turkey, thawed, may be substituted.

PEACH-MUSTARD-GLAZED PORK TENDERLOIN

MAKES: 8 servings ▪ **HANDS-ON TIME:** 25 min. ▪ **TOTAL TIME:** 1 hour

2   (1¼-lb.) pork tenderloins
½   tsp. table salt
½   tsp. freshly ground black pepper
2   Tbsp. olive oil
2   Tbsp. butter
1   large shallot, minced
½   cup peach preserves
⅓   cup bourbon
¼   tsp. dried crushed red pepper
2   Tbsp. country-style Dijon
      mustard
½   cup reduced-sodium fat-free
      chicken broth

1. Preheat oven to 400°. Sprinkle tenderloins with salt and black pepper. Cook in hot oil in a large ovenproof skillet over high heat 3 to 4 minutes on each side or until lightly browned.

2. Melt butter in a small skillet over medium-high heat; add shallot, and sauté 2 to 3 minutes or until tender. Remove from heat, and stir in peach preserves and next 3 ingredients. Cook over medium heat, stirring often, 1 minute or until preserves are melted. Pour mixture over tenderloins.

3. Bake at 400° for 20 minutes or until a meat thermometer inserted in thickest portion registers 145°. Transfer pork tenderloins to a cutting board, reserving pan drippings in skillet. Cover loosely with aluminum foil, and let stand 10 minutes before slicing.

4. Meanwhile, stir broth into reserved drippings, and cook over medium-high heat, stirring constantly, 5 minutes or until drippings are reduced by half. Serve with sliced tenderloins.

HOLIDAY TRADITION

Add a Southern touch to your Christmas dinner with this tangy glaze for pork tenderloin. Serve classic Southern side dishes such as green beans, grits, and squash casserole.

PORK ROAST
with Sweet Onion-Pumpkin Seed Relish

Be sure to ask your butcher to cut out the chine bone and french the rib rack for easy carving and an elegant presentation.

MAKES: 8 servings ▪ **HANDS-ON TIME:** 20 min. ▪ **TOTAL TIME:** 1 hour, 50 min.

1¼ tsp. table salt, divided
½ tsp. freshly ground black pepper
1 (5-lb.) 8-rib bone-in pork loin roast, chine bone removed
1 Tbsp. minced fresh rosemary
3 tsp. minced fresh thyme, divided
3 large sweet onions (about 2 lb.), cut into ½-inch-thick rings
2 Tbsp. olive oil
⅛ tsp. freshly ground black pepper
1 tsp. white wine vinegar
1 tsp. light brown sugar
¼ cup toasted pumpkin seeds

1. Preheat oven to 450°. Sprinkle 1 tsp. salt and ½ tsp. black pepper over pork; rub rosemary and 2 tsp. thyme over pork. Place pork in a lightly greased roasting pan.

2. Toss together onions, olive oil, ⅛ tsp. black pepper, and remaining ¼ tsp. salt until coated. Arrange onions around pork in pan.

3. Bake at 450° for 30 minutes; reduce oven temperature to 375°. Bake 50 more minutes or until a meat thermometer inserted into thickest portion registers 145°, stirring onions once. Transfer pork to a cutting board; cover loosely with aluminum foil, and let stand 10 minutes before slicing.

4. Meanwhile, coarsely chop onions; transfer to a medium bowl. Stir in vinegar, brown sugar, and remaining 1 tsp. thyme. Stir in toasted pumpkin seeds before serving. Serve pork with relish.

SPICY FRUIT-STUFFED PORK LOIN
with Roasted Pears and Onions
Adding dried crushed red pepper to the stuffing keeps this fruity dish savory and creates a fun flavor surprise.

MAKES: 8 to 10 servings ▪ **HANDS-ON TIME:** 1 hour ▪ **TOTAL TIME:** 2 hours, 20 min.

PORK LOIN

2 (7-oz.) packages mixed dried fruit bits
2 Tbsp. dark brown sugar
1 Tbsp. chopped fresh sage
¼ tsp. dried crushed red pepper
1 (4-lb.) boneless pork loin
1½ tsp. kosher salt, divided
1½ tsp. coarsely ground black pepper, divided
Kitchen string
2 Tbsp. olive oil

ROASTED PEARS AND ONIONS

6 firm, ripe Seckel pears*
2 Tbsp. butter, melted
2 tsp. fresh lemon juice
2 tsp. honey**
¼ tsp. finely chopped fresh rosemary
¼ tsp. kosher salt
¼ tsp. freshly ground black pepper
2 (10-oz.) packages cipollini onions, peeled

GLAZE

½ cup pear preserves

1. Prepare Pork Loin: Bring first 4 ingredients and 1 cup water to a boil in a small saucepan over medium-high heat. Cook 2 minutes, stirring once. Remove from heat, and cool completely (about 40 minutes).

2. Meanwhile, butterfly pork by making a lengthwise cut down center of 1 flat side, cutting to within ½ inch of other side. (Do not cut all the way through pork.) Open pork, forming a rectangle, and place between 2 sheets of heavy-duty plastic wrap. Flatten to ½-inch thickness using a meat mallet or rolling pin. Sprinkle with ½ tsp. each salt and black pepper.

3. Spoon fruit mixture over pork, leaving a ½-inch border around edges. Roll up pork, jelly-roll fashion, starting at 1 long side. Tie with string at 1½-inch intervals. Sprinkle with remaining 1 tsp. salt and 1 tsp. pepper.

4. Preheat oven to 375°. Brown pork in hot oil in a large roasting pan over medium-high heat until browned on all sides (about 2 to 3 minutes per side). Place pork seam side down.

5. Prepare Roasted Pears and Onions: Cut pears in half lengthwise, and remove core. Stir together butter and next 5 ingredients. Stir in onions; gently stir in pear halves. Spoon mixture around roast in roasting pan.

6. Bake at 375° for 1 hour to 1 hour and 5 minutes or until a meat thermometer inserted into thickest portion of stuffing registers 135°, stirring pear mixture halfway through. Cover with aluminum foil, and let stand 15 minutes.

7. Prepare Glaze: Microwave preserves in a microwave-safe bowl at HIGH 1 minute or until thoroughly heated. Pour warm preserves over pork. Slice pork, and serve with Roasted Pears and Onions and pan juices.

*3 firm, ripe Bartlett pears may be substituted. Core pears, and cut into 4 wedges each.
**Sugar may be substituted.

HONEY-BOURBON-GLAZED HAM

MAKES: 15 servings ▪ **HANDS-ON TIME:** 20 min. ▪ **TOTAL TIME:** 3 hours, 20 min.

1   (9¼-lb.) fully cooked,
      bone-in ham
40 whole cloves
½   cup firmly packed light brown
      sugar
½   cup bourbon
½   cup honey
⅓   cup Creole mustard
⅓   cup molasses
Garnish: fresh fruit

1. Preheat oven to 350°. Remove skin from ham, and trim fat to ¼-inch thickness. Make shallow cuts in fat 1 inch apart in a diamond pattern; insert cloves in centers of diamonds. Place ham in an aluminum foil-lined 13- x 9-inch pan.

2. Stir together brown sugar and next 4 ingredients; spoon over ham.

3. Bake at 350° on lower oven rack 2 hours and 30 minutes, basting with pan juices every 30 minutes. Shield ham with aluminum foil after 1 hour to prevent excessive browning, if necessary. Remove from oven, and let stand 30 minutes before serving.

Try this twist!

Honey-Bourbon Boneless Glazed Ham: Substitute 1 (4-lb.) smoked, fully cooked boneless ham for bone-in ham. Reduce cloves to 3 (do not insert into ham). Stir together brown sugar mixture as directed in Step 2; stir in cloves. Place ham in an aluminum foil-lined 13- x 9-inch pan. Pour sauce over ham. Bake as directed, reducing bake time to 1 hour, and basting after 30 minutes.

HONEY-CURRY-GLAZED LAMB

Consider ordering the lamb roasts from your butcher a few days ahead.

MAKES: 6 servings ▪ **HANDS-ON TIME:** 15 min. ▪ **TOTAL TIME:** 1 hour, 30 min., including Roasted Grapes and Cranberries

2 (8-rib) lamb rib roasts
(2½ lb. each), trimmed
1 Tbsp. red curry powder
1½ tsp. kosher salt
1½ tsp. freshly ground black pepper
5 Tbsp. olive oil
2 Tbsp. honey
Roasted Grapes and Cranberries

1. Preheat oven to 425°. Sprinkle lamb on all sides with curry powder, salt, and black pepper. Let stand 30 minutes.

2. Cook lamb in 1 Tbsp. hot oil in a 12-inch cast-iron skillet over medium heat 6 to 7 minutes, turning often to brown tops and sides. Place lamb, meat side up, in skillet. Stir together honey and remaining 4 Tbsp. olive oil; brush mixture on tops and sides of lamb.

3. Bake at 425° for 15 to 18 minutes or until a meat thermometer inserted into thickest portion registers 130° (rare). Remove lamb from oven; let stand 10 minutes. Cut into chops, and serve with Roasted Grapes and Cranberries.

Roasted Grapes and Cranberries

*This accompaniment pairs well with both lamb and pork dishes.
You can also add it to a cheese tray for a unique touch.*

MAKES: 6 servings ▪ **HANDS-ON TIME:** 5 min. ▪ **TOTAL TIME:** 20 min.

6 to 8 seedless red grape clusters
(about 1 lb.)
1 cup fresh cranberries
1 Tbsp. olive oil
1 tsp. chopped fresh rosemary

1. Preheat oven to 400°. Place grape clusters on a 15- x 10-inch jelly-roll pan. Stir together cranberries and next 2 ingredients. Spoon mixture over grape clusters.

2. Bake at 400° for 15 to 18 minutes or until grapes begin to blister and cranberries start to pop, shaking pan occasionally. Serve immediately, or let stand up to 4 hours.

HERB-AND-POTATO CHIP-CRUSTED BEEF TENDERLOIN

Let your guests in on the secret to this beef tenderloin's crispy herb coating and rich, salty seasoning: potato chips!

MAKES: 6 to 8 servings ▪ **HANDS-ON TIME:** 40 min. ▪ **TOTAL TIME:** 2 hours, 20 min.

1   (4- to 5-lb.) beef tenderloin, trimmed
3   tsp. kosher salt, divided
¾   cup panko (Japanese breadcrumbs)
3   garlic cloves, pressed
2   tsp. coarsely ground black pepper, divided
3   Tbsp. olive oil, divided
1¼   cups crushed plain kettle-cooked potato chips
¼   cup finely chopped fresh parsley
1   Tbsp. finely chopped fresh thyme
1   bay leaf, crushed
1   large egg white, lightly beaten
1   Tbsp. Dijon mustard
Garnish: sage leaves

1. Sprinkle tenderloin with 2 tsp. salt. Let stand 30 to 45 minutes.

2. Meanwhile, sauté panko, garlic, 1 tsp. black pepper, and remaining 1 tsp. salt in 1 Tbsp. hot oil in a skillet over medium heat 2 to 3 minutes or until deep golden brown. Let cool completely (about 10 minutes). Stir in potato chips and next 4 ingredients.

3. Preheat oven to 400°. Pat tenderloin dry with paper towels, and sprinkle with remaining 1 tsp. black pepper. Brown beef in remaining 2 Tbsp. hot oil in a roasting pan over medium-high heat until browned on all sides (about 2 to 3 minutes per side). Transfer tenderloin to a wire rack in an aluminum foil-lined jelly-roll pan. Let stand 10 minutes.

4. Spread mustard over tenderloin. Press panko mixture onto top and sides of tenderloin.

5. Bake at 400° for 40 to 45 minutes or until coating is crisp and a meat thermometer inserted into thickest portion of tenderloin registers 130° (rare). Let stand 10 minutes.

Note: *We tested with Lay's Kettle Cooked Original Potato Chips. For medium-rare, cook tenderloin to 135°; for medium, cook to 150°.*

DECADENT DESSERTS

From cakes to cookies, satisfy
everyone's sweet tooth with these
scrumptious recipes. They make
a delicious ending to any meal or are
just perfect for a holiday gift.

PEANUT BUTTER TRUFFLES

MAKES: about 2 dozen ▪ **HANDS-ON TIME:** 20 min. ▪ **TOTAL TIME:** 3 hours, 30 min.

1 (12-oz.) package semisweet chocolate morsels
½ cup whipping cream
3 Tbsp. creamy peanut butter
¾ cup finely chopped, lightly salted roasted peanuts
Wax paper

1. Microwave first 3 ingredients in a medium-size microwave-safe bowl at HIGH 1 to 1½ minutes or until melted and smooth, stirring at 30-second intervals. Let cool 10 minutes.

2. Beat chocolate mixture at medium speed with an electric mixer 1 to 2 minutes or until whipped and smooth. Cover and chill 2 hours or until firm.

3. Shape chocolate mixture into 1-inch balls, using a small ice-cream scoop. Roll in chopped peanuts. (If chocolate mixture becomes too soft to shape, refrigerate until firm.) Place on wax paper-lined baking sheets. Chill 1 hour before serving. Store truffles in an airtight container in refrigerator up to 5 days.

LINZER COOKIES

MAKES: 3 dozen ▪ **HANDS-ON TIME:** 25 min. ▪ **TOTAL TIME:** 1 hour, 40 min.

1¼ cups butter, softened
1 cup powdered sugar, sifted
2½ cups all-purpose flour
½ cup finely chopped pecans, toasted
1 tsp. grated lemon rind
¼ tsp. salt
¼ tsp. ground cloves
¼ tsp. ground cinnamon
¼ cup seedless raspberry jam
Powdered sugar

1. Beat butter at medium speed with an electric mixer until creamy; gradually add 1 cup powdered sugar, beating until light and fluffy.

2. Combine flour and next 5 ingredients; gradually add to butter mixture, beating just until blended.

3. Preheat oven to 325°. Divide dough into 2 portions. Cover; chill 1 hour.

4. Roll each portion to ⅛-inch thickness on a lightly floured surface. Cut with a 3-inch star-shaped cutter; cut centers out of half of cookies with 1½-inch star-shaped cutter. Place all cookies on lightly greased baking sheets.

5. Bake at 325° for 15 minutes; remove to wire racks to cool completely.

6. Spread all large solid cookies and half of small cookies with jam; sprinkle remaining cookies with powdered sugar. Top each large solid cookie with a hollow cookie and each small cookie with jam with a small plain cookie.

PEANUT BUTTER
TRUFFLES

LINZER
COOKIES

RED VELVET CUPCAKES
(PAGE 132)

PEAR DUMPLINGS

MAKES: 6 servings ■ **HANDS-ON TIME:** 40 min. ■ **TOTAL TIME:** 1 hour, 20 min.

3   cups all-purpose flour
2   tsp. baking powder
1   tsp. table salt
1   cup shortening
¾   cup milk
6   ripe Bosc pears
¼   cup firmly packed light
    brown sugar
1½ cups chopped macadamia nuts
1   tsp. ground cinnamon
¼   cup butter, softened
1½ cups granulated sugar
Orange peel strips of 1 medium
    orange
1   (3-inch) piece fresh ginger
1   Tbsp. butter
Garnishes: orange slices, cinnamon
    sticks, fresh mint

1. Preheat oven to 375°. Stir together first 3 ingredients; cut shortening into flour mixture with a pastry blender or fork until crumbly. Gradually add milk, stirring just until dry ingredients are moistened.

2. Turn dough out onto a lightly floured surface, and knead lightly 4 to 5 times. Shape into a 12-inch log. Cut log into 6 (2-inch) pieces. Shape each into a disk, and roll each into an 8-inch circle on a lightly floured surface.

3. Peel pears, reserving peels. Core each pear from bottom, leaving top 2 inches and stems intact.

4. Stir together brown sugar and next 2 ingredients; spoon about 1½ Tbsp. brown sugar mixture into each pear cavity, pressing firmly. Sprinkle remaining sugar mixture in center of pastry circles (about 1½ Tbsp. each). Place 1 pear in center of each pastry circle. Dot pears with ¼ cup softened butter. Press dough around pears with palms of hands, sealing around stem. Place in a lightly greased 13- x 9-inch baking dish.

5. Bake at 375° for 40 to 50 minutes, shielding with aluminum foil after 30 minutes to prevent excessive browning, if necessary.

6. Bring granulated sugar, next 3 ingredients, reserved pear peels, and 1½ cups water to a boil over medium-high heat, stirring constantly. Boil, stirring constantly, 1 minute or until sugar dissolves. Reduce heat to low. Cook, stirring occasionally, 5 minutes. Pour through a wire-mesh strainer into a bowl; discard solids. Pour syrup over dumplings. Serve immediately.

WRAP IT UP

Present friends and neighbors with a gift box filled with fresh pears. Attach this recipe to the box for the perfect presentation.

APPLE-CHERRY COBBLER WITH PINWHEEL BISCUITS

MAKES: 8 to 10 servings ▪ **HANDS-ON TIME:** 1 hour ▪ **TOTAL TIME:** 1 hour, 15 min.

APPLE-CHERRY FILLING

8   large Braeburn apples, peeled and cut into ½-inch-thick wedges (about 4 ½ lb.)
2   cups granulated sugar
¼   cup all-purpose flour
¼   cup butter
1   (12-oz.) package frozen cherries, thawed and well drained
1   tsp. lemon zest
⅓   cup fresh lemon juice
1   tsp. ground cinnamon

PINWHEEL BISCUITS

2¼ cups all-purpose flour
¼   cup granulated sugar
2¼ tsp. baking powder
¾   tsp. salt
¾   cup cold butter, cut into pieces
⅔   cup milk
⅔   cup firmly packed light brown sugar
2   Tbsp. butter, melted
¼   cup finely chopped roasted unsalted almonds

1. Prepare Apple-Cherry Filling: Preheat oven to 425°. Toss together first 3 ingredients. Melt ¼ cup butter in a large skillet over medium-high heat; add apple mixture. Cook, stirring often, 20 to 25 minutes or until apples are tender and syrup thickens. Remove from heat; stir in cherries and next 3 ingredients. Spoon apple mixture into a lightly greased 3-qt. baking dish. Bake at 425° for 12 minutes, placing a baking sheet on oven rack directly below baking dish to catch any drips.

2. Prepare Pinwheel Biscuits: Stir together 2 ¼ cups flour and next 3 ingredients in a large bowl. Cut butter into flour mixture with a pastry blender or fork until crumbly; stir in milk. Turn dough out onto a lightly floured surface; knead 4 to 5 times. Roll dough into a 12-inch square. Combine brown sugar and 2 Tbsp. melted butter; sprinkle over dough, patting gently. Sprinkle with almonds. Roll up, jelly-roll fashion; pinch seams and ends to seal. Cut roll into 12 (1-inch) slices. Place slices in a single layer on top of apple mixture.

3. Bake at 425° for 15 to 17 minutes or until biscuits are golden.

AMBROSIA CHESS TARTS

MAKES: 14 tarts ▪ **HANDS-ON TIME:** 30 min. ▪ **TOTAL TIME:** 2 hours, 20 min.

2   (14.1-oz.) packages refrigerated
    piecrusts*
1½ cups sugar
1   Tbsp. all-purpose flour
1   Tbsp. plain white cornmeal
½   tsp. table salt
4   large eggs
½   cup cream of coconut
⅓   cup butter, melted
¼   cup fresh lemon juice
1   cup sweetened flaked coconut
1   (8-oz.) can crushed pineapple
2   Tbsp. orange zest
Toppings: toasted coconut,
    sweetened whipped cream,
    orange sections, fresh
    rosemary sprigs

1. Preheat oven to 450°. Cut piecrusts into 14 (4½-inch) rounds. Press each dough round into a lightly greased 3½-inch brioche mold, pressing up sides. Fold dough over edge of molds, and pinch to secure. Arrange molds on a baking sheet. Bake 7 to 8 minutes or until lightly browned. Cool completely on baking sheet on a wire rack (about 30 minutes). Reduce oven temperature to 350°.

2. Meanwhile, whisk together sugar and next 3 ingredients in a large bowl; add eggs and next 3 ingredients, and whisk until blended. Stir in coconut and next 2 ingredients. Spoon coconut mixture into cooled pastry shells, filling almost full.

3. Bake at 350° for 22 to 25 minutes or until golden brown and centers of tarts are almost set. (Filling will continue to cook as it cools.) Cool tarts completely on baking sheet on wire rack (about 1 hour). Loosen tarts from molds using a small knife; remove tarts from molds. Serve with desired toppings.

2 (8- or 10-oz.) packages frozen tart shells may be substituted. Bake as directed in Step 1.

HOLIDAY TRADITION

Adding ambrosia to the Christmas day dinner is a tradition among many families in the South. The biggest debate can be over whether or not to add marshmallows or pecans. These delicious Ambrosia Chess Tarts add a festive twist on this holiday classic.

BOURBON-CREAM CHEESE BROWNIES

MAKES: 16 brownies ▪ **HANDS-ON TIME:** 30 min. ▪ **TOTAL TIME:** 2 hours, 10 min.

4 (1-oz.) unsweetened chocolate
 baking squares
¾ cup butter
½ cup firmly packed light brown
 sugar
1¾ cups granulated sugar, divided
4 large eggs, divided
1 tsp. vanilla extract
⅛ tsp. table salt
1 cup all-purpose flour
1 (8-oz.) package cream cheese,
 softened
2 Tbsp. all-purpose flour
¼ cup bourbon

1. Preheat oven to 350°. Line bottom and sides of a 9-inch square pan with aluminum foil, allowing 2 to 3 inches to extend over sides; lightly grease foil.

2. Microwave chocolate squares and butter in a large microwave-safe bowl at HIGH 1½ to 2 minutes or until melted and smooth, stirring at 30-second intervals. Whisk in brown sugar and 1½ cups granulated sugar. Add 3 eggs, 1 at a time, whisking just until blended after each addition. Whisk in vanilla, salt, and 1 cup flour. Spread half of batter in prepared pan.

3. Beat cream cheese at medium speed with an electric mixer until smooth; add 2 Tbsp. flour and remaining ¼ cup granulated sugar, beating until blended. Add bourbon and remaining 1 egg, beating until blended.

4. Slowly pour cream cheese mixture over batter in pan; top with remaining batter, and swirl together gently with a knife.

5. Bake at 350° for 40 to 45 minutes or until a wooden pick inserted in center comes out with a few moist crumbs. Cool completely in pan on a wire rack (about 1 hour). Lift brownies from pan, using foil sides as handles. Gently remove foil; and cut brownies into 16 squares.

BOURBON BALLS

MAKES: about 5 dozen ▪ **HANDS-ON TIME:** 30 min. ▪ **TOTAL TIME:** 53 min.

1 (12-oz.) package vanilla wafers,
 finely crushed
1 cup toasted chopped pecans
¾ cup powdered sugar
2 Tbsp. unsweetened cocoa
½ cup bourbon
2½ Tbsp. light corn syrup
Powdered sugar

1. Stir together wafers and next 3 ingredients in a large bowl until well blended.

2. Stir together bourbon and corn syrup in a small bowl until well blended. Pour bourbon mixture over wafer mixture, stirring until blended. Shape into 1-inch balls; roll in powdered sugar. Cover and chill up to 2 weeks.

BOURBON-CREAM
CHEESE BROWNIES

DOUBLE CHOCOLATE
CHIP COOKIES
(PAGE 131)

BOURBON BALLS

peace
love AND joy

RED VELVET BROWNIES

RED VELVET BROWNIES

MAKES: about 2 dozen ▪ **HANDS-ON TIME:** 20 min. ▪ **TOTAL TIME:** 1 hour, 50 min.

1　(4-oz.) bittersweet chocolate
　　baking bar, chopped
¾　cup butter
2¼　cups sugar, divided
4　large eggs
1　(1-oz.) bottle red liquid food
　　coloring
¼　tsp. peppermint extract
2　tsp. vanilla extract, divided
1½　cups all-purpose flour
⅛　tsp. table salt
½　(8-oz.) package cream cheese,
　　softened
2　large egg whites
2　Tbsp. all-purpose flour

1. Preheat oven to 350°. Line bottom and sides of a 13- x 9-inch pan with aluminum foil, allowing 2 inches to extend over sides; lightly grease. Microwave chocolate and butter in a microwave-safe bowl at HIGH 1½ to 2 minutes or until melted and smooth, stirring at 30-second intervals. Whisk in 2 cups sugar. Add eggs, 1 at a time, whisking just until blended after each addition. Add food coloring, peppermint extract, and 1 tsp. vanilla. Gently stir in 1½ cups flour and salt. Pour into pan.

2. Beat cream cheese and remaining ¼ cup sugar at medium speed with an electric mixer until fluffy. Add egg whites and remaining 1 tsp. vanilla; beat until blended. Stir in 2 Tbsp. flour until smooth. Drop by heaping tablespoonfuls over batter in pan; gently swirl with a knife. Bake at 350° for 30 to 32 minutes. Cool completely in pan on a wire rack (about 1 hour). Lift from pan, using foil sides as handles. Remove foil; cut into squares.

DOUBLE CHOCOLATE CHIP COOKIES

MAKES: 2½ dozen ▪ **HANDS-ON TIME:** 45 min. ▪ **TOTAL TIME:** 5 hours, 48 min., including ganache

¾　cup butter, softened
¾　cup granulated sugar
¾　cup firmly packed dark
　　brown sugar
2　large eggs
1½　tsp. vanilla extract
2½　cups all-purpose flour
1　tsp. baking soda
¾　tsp. salt
1　(12-oz.) package semisweet
　　chocolate morsels
Parchment paper

BOURBON GANACHE:
1　(12-oz.) package semisweet
　　chocolate morsels
½　cup whipping cream
3　Tbsp. bourbon
3　Tbsp. butter, softened
½　tsp. vanilla extract

1. Preheat oven to 350°. Beat butter and sugars at medium speed with a heavy-duty electric stand mixer until creamy. Add eggs, 1 at a time, beating just until blended after each addition. Add vanilla, beating until blended.

2. Combine flour and next 2 ingredients; gradually add to butter mixture, beating at low speed just until blended. Stir in morsels just until combined. Drop dough by level spoonfuls onto parchment paper-lined baking sheets, using a small cookie scoop.

3. Bake at 350° for 12 minutes or until golden brown. Remove from baking sheets to wire racks, and cool completely (about 30 minutes).

4. Prepare Ganache: Microwave chocolate morsels and whipping cream in a 2-qt. microwave-safe bowl at MEDIUM 2½ minutes or until chocolate begins to melt, stirring at 30-second intervals. Whisk in bourbon, butter, and vanilla. Cover and chill, stirring occasionally, 1 hour and 30 minutes or until thickened to a spreadable consistency.

5. Spread Bourbon Ganache on flat side of half of cookies (about 1 Tbsp. per cookie); top with remaining cookies. Cover and chill cookies 2 hours or until ganache is firm.

RED VELVET CUPCAKES

MAKES: 2 dozen ■ HANDS-ON TIME: 25 min. ■ TOTAL TIME: 2 hours, 18 min., including frosting

¾ cup butter, softened

1½ cups sugar

3 large eggs

1 (1-oz.) bottle red liquid food coloring

1 tsp. vanilla extract

2½ cups all-purpose flour

3 Tbsp. unsweetened cocoa

½ tsp. salt

1 cup buttermilk

1 Tbsp. white vinegar

1 tsp. baking soda

24 paper baking cups

White Chocolate-Amaretto Frosting

Parchment paper

½ cup (4 oz.) white fondant

¾ cup powdered sugar

1 Tbsp. milk

Coarse sanding sugar

Garnish: red candy sprinkles

1. Preheat oven to 350°. Beat butter at medium speed with an electric mixer until fluffy; gradually add sugar, beating well. Add eggs, 1 at a time, beating until blended after each addition. Stir in food coloring and vanilla, blending well.

2. Combine flour, cocoa, and salt. Stir together buttermilk, vinegar, and baking soda in a 4-cup liquid measuring cup. (Mixture will bubble.) Add flour mixture to butter mixture alternately with buttermilk mixture, beginning and ending with flour mixture. Beat at low speed until blended after each addition. Place paper baking cups in 2 (12-cup) muffin pans; spoon batter into cups, filling three-fourths full.

3. Bake at 350° for 18 to 20 minutes or until a wooden pick inserted in centers comes out clean. Remove cupcakes from pans to wire racks, and cool completely (about 45 minutes).

4. Pipe White Chocolate-Amaretto Frosting onto cupcakes.

5. To make cupcake toppers, roll out fondant to ¼-inch thickness on parchment paper. Transfer to a baking sheet; cut with a small snowflake- or star-shaped cutter, reroll fondant if necessary. Make glaze by mixing powdered sugar and milk until well blended; brush toppers with a light layer of glaze and sprinkle with coarse sanding sugar. Let stand 1 hour or until set. Place toppers on cupcakes.

White Chocolate-Amaretto Frosting

MAKES: 4 cups ■ HANDS-ON TIME: 20 min. ■ TOTAL TIME: 50 min.

2 (4-oz.) white chocolate baking bars

⅓ cup heavy cream

1 cup butter, softened

6 cups sifted powdered sugar

¼ cup amaretto liqueur

1. Break chocolate baking bars into pieces. Microwave chocolate pieces and cream in a microwave-safe container at MEDIUM (50% power) 1 minute or until melted and smooth, stirring at 30-second intervals. (Do not overheat.) Cool to room temperature (about 30 minutes).

2. Beat butter and 1 cup powdered sugar at low speed with an electric mixer until blended. Add remaining 5 cups powdered sugar alternately with amaretto liqueur, beating at low speed until blended after each addition. Add white chocolate mixture; beat at medium speed until spreading consistency.

RUM-GLAZED SWEET POTATO CAKES

MAKES: 3 dozen ▪ **HANDS-ON TIME:** 40 min. ▪ **TOTAL TIME:** 1 hour, 30 min.

¾ cup golden raisins

⅓ cup dark rum

4 large eggs, at room temperature

2 cups granulated sugar

1 cup vegetable oil

2 tsp. vanilla extract

2 cups pureed roasted sweet potatoes

3 cups all-purpose flour

1½ tsp. ground cinnamon

1 tsp. baking powder

1 tsp. baking soda

½ tsp. fine sea salt

½ tsp. ground nutmeg

¾ cup buttermilk

½ cup firmly packed dark brown sugar

¼ cup butter

3 Tbsp. whipping cream

½ cup finely chopped toasted pecans

1. Stir together first 2 ingredients. Let stand 30 minutes.

2. Meanwhile, beat eggs and granulated sugar at high speed with an electric mixer 2 to 4 minutes or until thick and pale. Add oil and vanilla, beating at low speed just until blended. Add sweet potato puree, beating just until blended and stopping to scrape down sides as needed.

3. Preheat oven to 350°. Sift together flour and next 5 ingredients; add to egg mixture alternately with buttermilk, beginning and ending with flour mixture. Beat at low speed just until blended after each addition. Drain raisins, reserving rum. Fold raisins into batter. Spoon batter into 3 lightly greased 12-cup Bundt brownie pans, filling each three-fourths full.

4. Bake at 350° for 14 to 16 minutes or until a wooden pick inserted in center comes out clean. Cool in pans on lightly greased wire racks 5 minutes. Remove from pans to wire racks.

5. Meanwhile, bring brown sugar and next 2 ingredients to a boil in a heavy saucepan over medium-high heat. Boil, stirring constantly, 3 minutes or until mixture begins to thicken to a syrup-like consistency. Remove from heat; stir in reserved rum.

6. Pierce tops of cakes multiple times using a wooden pick. Dip top halves of cakes in glaze, and hold 1 to 2 seconds (to allow glaze to soak into cakes). Place, glazed sides up, on lightly greased racks. Sprinkle each cake with pecans.

Tip: To puree roasted sweet potatoes, peel potatoes as soon as they are slightly cool. Press pulp through a wire-mesh strainer with the back of a spoon. You'll need to roast about 1½ lb. potatoes for 2 cups puree.

BROWN SUGAR-BOURBON BUNDT

MAKES: 12 servings ■ HANDS-ON TIME: 20 min. ■ TOTAL TIME: 2 hours, 35 min.

1   cup butter, softened
½   cup shortening
1   (16-oz.) package light brown
      sugar
5   large eggs
1   (5-oz.) can evaporated milk
½   cup bourbon
3   cups all-purpose flour
½   tsp. baking powder
½   tsp. table salt
1   Tbsp. vanilla bean paste
2   Tbsp. powdered sugar
Garnishes: candied oranges,
      magnolia leaves

1. Preheat oven to 325°. Beat butter and shortening at medium speed with a heavy-duty electric stand mixer until creamy. Gradually add brown sugar, beating at medium speed until light and creamy. Add eggs, 1 at a time, beating just until blended after each addition.

2. Stir together evaporated milk and bourbon in a bowl. Stir together flour, baking powder, and salt in another bowl. Add flour mixture to butter mixture alternately with milk mixture, beginning and ending with flour mixture. Beat at low speed just until blended after each addition. Stir in vanilla bean paste. Pour batter into a greased and floured 10-inch (12-cup) Bundt pan.

3. Bake at 325° for 1 hour and 5 minutes to 1 hour and 10 minutes or until a long wooden pick inserted in center comes out clean. Cool in pan on a wire rack 10 to 15 minutes; remove from pan to wire rack. Cool completely (about 1 hour). Dust lightly with powdered sugar.

WRAP IT UP

Package a homemade cake in a decorative cake box or on a pretty platter to give to a friend or teacher this Christmas. Best of all, it can be made ahead and frozen for up to a month.

BLACK FOREST POUND CAKE

This decadent dessert is an easy, one-pan twist on the traditional layered cake.

MAKES: 10 servings ▪ **HANDS-ON TIME:** 30 min. ▪ **TOTAL TIME:** 3 hours, 15 min., including sauce

⅔ cup butter, softened
1⅓ cups granulated sugar
⅔ cup firmly packed dark brown
    sugar
4 large eggs
1¼ tsp. vanilla extract, divided
1½ cups cake flour
½ cup unsweetened cocoa
½ tsp. salt
¼ tsp. baking soda
¾ cup sour cream
3 (1-oz.) bittersweet chocolate
    baking squares, finely
    chopped
Cherry Sauce
1¼ cups heavy cream
1 Tbsp. granulated sugar
Shaved bittersweet chocolate

1. Preheat oven to 325°. Beat butter at medium speed with a heavy-duty electric stand mixer until creamy. Gradually add 1⅓ cups granulated sugar and brown sugar, beating until light and fluffy (about 5 minutes). Add eggs, 1 at a time, beating just until blended after each addition. Beat in 1 tsp. vanilla.

2. Whisk together flour and next 3 ingredients. Add to butter mixture alternately with sour cream, beginning and ending with flour mixture. Beat at low speed just until blended after each addition. Stir in chopped chocolate.

3. Pour batter into a greased and floured 10-inch round cake pan (with sides that are 3 inches high).

4. Bake at 325° for 1 hour and 10 minutes to 1 hour and 20 minutes or until a wooden pick inserted in center comes out clean. Cool in pan on a wire rack 15 minutes. Remove from pan to wire rack; cool completely (about 1 hour).

5. Place cake on a serving plate or cake stand. Slowly pour Cherry Sauce over cake. Beat heavy cream, 1 Tbsp. granulated sugar, and remaining ¼ tsp. vanilla at medium-high speed until soft peaks form. Dollop whipped cream onto cake, and sprinkle with shaved chocolate.

Cherry Sauce

We used Kirsch, a fruit brandy made with sweet cherries, but the brandy in your liquor cabinet will work just fine. This sauce is also delicious over an ice-cream sundae. Try it on pancakes and waffles, too.

MAKES: 1½ cups ▪ **HANDS-ON TIME:** 20 min. ▪ **TOTAL TIME:** 1 hour, 20 min.

2 (12-oz.) packages frozen cherries
⅓ cup sugar
⅓ cup cold water
3 tsp. cornstarch
2 Tbsp. cherry liqueur or brandy
Pinch of salt

Stir together first 4 ingredients in a medium saucepan. Cook over medium-low heat, stirring often, 12 to 15 minutes or until thickened. Remove from heat, and stir in remaining ingredients. Cool completely (about 1 hour).

CRANBERRY-APPLE-PUMPKIN BUNDT

MAKES: 12 servings ▪ **HANDS-ON TIME:** 30 min. ▪ **TOTAL TIME:** 4 hours, 40 min., including toppings

1½ cups peeled and diced Granny
    Smith apples
2 Tbsp. butter, melted
½ cup finely chopped sweetened
    dried cranberries
½ cup firmly packed light brown
    sugar
3 Tbsp. all-purpose flour
¾ cup finely chopped toasted pecans
2 cups granulated sugar
1 cup butter, softened
4 large eggs
1 (15-oz.) can pumpkin
1 Tbsp. vanilla extract
3 cups all-purpose flour
2 tsp. baking powder
2 tsp. pumpkin pie spice
½ tsp. baking soda
Maple Glaze
Sugared Pecans and Pepitas

1. Preheat oven to 325°. Toss diced apples in 2 Tbsp. melted butter to coat in a medium bowl; add cranberries and next 3 ingredients, and toss until well blended.

2. Beat granulated sugar and 1 cup softened butter at medium speed with an electric mixer until light and fluffy. Add eggs, 1 at a time, beating just until blended after each addition. Add pumpkin and vanilla; beat just until blended.

3. Stir together 3 cups flour and next 3 ingredients. Gradually add flour mixture to butter mixture, beating at low speed just until blended after each addition. Spoon half of batter into a greased and floured 10-inch (12-cup) Bundt pan. Spoon apple mixture over batter, leaving a ½-inch border around outer edge. Spoon remaining batter over apple mixture.

4. Bake at 325° for 1 hour and 10 minutes to 1 hour and 20 minutes or until a long wooden pick inserted in center comes out clean. Cool in pan on a wire rack 15 minutes. Remove from pan to wire rack; cool completely (about 2 hours).

5. Spoon hot Maple Glaze onto cooled cake. Arrange pecans and pepitas on top of cake.

Sugared Pecans and Pepitas

MAKES: 1½ cups ▪ **HANDS-ON TIME:** 5 min. ▪ **TOTAL TIME:** 47 min.

1 cup pecan halves and pieces
½ cup roasted, salted shelled
    pepitas (pumpkin seeds)
2 Tbsp. butter, melted
2 Tbsp. sugar

Preheat oven to 350°. Stir together first 3 ingredients. Spread in a single layer in a 13- x 9-inch pan. Bake 12 to 15 minutes or until toasted and fragrant, stirring halfway through. Remove from oven; toss with sugar. Cool completely in pan on a wire rack (about 30 minutes).

Maple Glaze

MAKES: 1 cup ▪ **HANDS-ON TIME:** 10 min. ▪ **TOTAL TIME:** 10 min.

½ cup pure maple syrup
2 Tbsp. butter
1 Tbsp. milk
1 tsp. vanilla extract
1 cup powdered sugar

Bring first 3 ingredients to a boil in a small saucepan over medium-high heat, stirring constantly; boil, stirring constantly, 2 minutes. Remove from heat; whisk in vanilla. Gradually whisk in sugar until smooth; stir gently 3 to 5 minutes or until mixture begins to thicken and cool slightly. Use immediately.

TIRAMISÙ LAYER CAKE

MAKES: 10 to 12 servings ▪ **HANDS-ON TIME:** 45 min. ▪ **TOTAL TIME:** 7 hours, 20 min., including syrup and frosting

TIRAMISÙ CAKE LAYERS
½ cup butter, softened
½ cup shortening
2 cups sugar
⅔ cup milk
3 cups all-purpose flour
1 Tbsp. baking powder
1 tsp. salt
1 Tbsp. vanilla bean paste*
1 tsp. almond extract
6 large egg whites
Garnishes: raspberries, strawberries, red currants, fresh mint

COFFEE SYRUP
½ cup sugar
⅔ cup strong brewed coffee
¼ cup brandy

MASCARPONE FROSTING
2 (8-oz.) packages mascarpone cheese
3 cups heavy cream
1 Tbsp. vanilla extract
⅔ cup sugar

1. Prepare Tiramisù Cake Layers: Preheat oven to 350°. Beat butter and shortening at medium speed with an electric mixer until fluffy; gradually add sugar, beating well.

2. Stir together milk and ⅔ cup water. Combine flour and next 2 ingredients; add to butter mixture alternately with milk mixture, beginning and ending with flour mixture. Beat at low speed just until blended after each addition. Stir in vanilla bean paste and almond extract.

3. Beat egg whites at high speed until stiff peaks form, and fold into batter. Spoon batter into 3 greased and floured 8-inch round cake pans.

4. Bake at 350° for 25 to 30 minutes or until a wooden pick inserted in center comes out clean. Cool in pans on wire racks 10 minutes; remove from pans to wire racks, and cool completely (about 1 hour).

5. Prepare Coffee Syrup: Combine sugar and ⅓ cup water in a microwave-safe bowl. Microwave at HIGH 1½ minutes or until sugar dissolves, stirring at 30-second intervals. Stir in coffee and brandy. Cool 1 hour.

6. Prepare Mascarpone Frosting: Stir mascarpone cheese in a large bowl just until blended. Beat cream and vanilla at low speed with an electric mixer until foamy; increase speed to medium-high and gradually add sugar, beating until stiff peaks form. (Do not overbeat or cream will be grainy.) Gently fold whipped cream mixture into mascarpone cheese. Use immediately.

7. Pierce cake layers with a wooden pick, making holes 1 inch apart. Brush or spoon Coffee Syrup over layers.

8. Place 1 cake layer, brushed side up, on a cake stand or serving plate. Spread top with 1⅓ cups Mascarpone Frosting. Top with second cake layer, brushed side up, and spread with 1⅓ cups Mascarpone Frosting. Top with remaining cake layer, brushed side up. Spread top and sides of cake with remaining Mascarpone Frosting. Chill 4 hours before serving.

*Vanilla extract may be substituted.

PEPPERMINT-HOT CHOCOLATE CAKE

MAKES: 10 to 12 servings ■ HANDS-ON TIME: 40 min. ■ TOTAL TIME: 2 hours, 25 min., including filling and frosting

PEPPERMINT-HOT CHOCOLATE CAKE LAYERS

½ cup boiling water
1 (4-oz.) milk chocolate baking bar, chopped
1 cup butter, softened
2 cups sugar
4 large eggs, separated
1 tsp. vanilla extract
2 cups all-purpose flour
¼ cup unsweetened cocoa
1 tsp. baking soda
1 tsp. table salt
1 cup buttermilk
Fudge Filling
Peppermint Cream Frosting
Garnishes: French vanilla cream-filled rolled wafer cookies dusted with powdered sugar, hard peppermint candies, fresh mint sprig

FUDGE FILLING

1 (14-oz.) can sweetened condensed milk
1 (12-oz.) package semisweet chocolate morsels
¼ tsp. peppermint extract

PEPPERMINT CREAM FROSTING

1 (7-oz.) jar marshmallow crème
1 (8-oz.) container frozen whipped topping, thawed
⅛ tsp. peppermint extract

1. Prepare Peppermint-Hot Chocolate Cake Layers: Preheat oven to 350°. Grease and flour 3 (8-inch) round cake pans.

2. Pour boiling water over chocolate in a small heatproof bowl. Stir until chocolate is melted and smooth. Cool to room temperature (about 30 minutes).

3. Beat butter at medium speed with a heavy-duty electric stand mixer until creamy; gradually add sugar, beating until light and fluffy. Add egg yolks, 1 at a time, beating until blended after each addition. Add melted chocolate and vanilla, beating until blended. Combine flour and next 3 ingredients; add to butter mixture alternately with buttermilk, beginning and ending with flour mixture. Beat at low speed just until blended after each addition.

4. Beat egg whites at medium speed until soft peaks form; gently fold into batter. Pour batter into prepared pans.

5. Bake at 350° for 20 to 30 minutes or until a wooden pick inserted in center comes out clean. Cool in pans on wire racks 10 minutes; remove from pans to wire racks, and cool completely (about 40 minutes).

6. Prepare Fudge Filling: Combine sweetened condensed milk and chocolate morsels in a saucepan, and cook over medium-low heat, stirring constantly, 4 to 6 minutes or until chocolate is melted and smooth. Remove from heat; stir in peppermint extract. Cool filling to room temperature (about 20 minutes).

7. Prepare Peppermint Cream Frosting: Beat marshmallow crème, whipped topping, and peppermint extract at high speed with an electric mixer 1 to 2 minutes or until glossy, stiff peaks form.

8. Spread Fudge Filling between cake layers. Spread Peppermint Cream frosting on top and sides of cake.

Note: *We tested with Nielsen-Massey Pure Peppermint Extract.*

WHITE CHOCOLATE RUSSE

MAKES: 12 servings ▪ **HANDS-ON TIME:** 30 min. ▪ **TOTAL TIME:** 4 hours, 30 min.

4   (3.4-oz.) packages fat-free white chocolate instant pudding mix
3½ cups whole milk
2   tsp. orange zest
1   Tbsp. orange liqueur or orange juice, divided
1   tsp. vanilla extract
1   cup whipping cream, whipped
24 ladyfingers (2 [3-oz.] packages)
Garnishes: raspberries, powdered sugar, fresh mint leaves, white chocolate curls

1. Prepare packages of pudding mix according to package directions, using 3½ cups whole milk instead of skim milk. Stir in orange zest, orange liqueur, and vanilla. Gently fold in whipped cream.

2. Line bottom and sides of a 9-inch springform pan with ladyfingers. Spoon pudding mixture into pan. Cover and chill at least 4 hours or until dessert is set.

3. Place dessert on a serving platter; carefully remove sides of pan.

Note: Here's an easy way to arrange ladyfingers in the springform pan: Simply remove rows of connected ladyfingers intact from their package, and unfold them into the bottom of pan, and then again around sides of pan.

WHITE CHOCOLATE-CRANBERRY CHEESECAKE

MAKES: 6 to 8 servings ▪ **HANDS-ON TIME:** 35 min. ▪ **TOTAL TIME:** 12 hours, 40 min., plus 1 day for chilling

CRANBERRY TOPPING

1   (12-oz.) package fresh
        cranberries
1   cup sugar
½   cup seedless raspberry jam
Garnish: fresh mint leaves

PIECRUST

1   (9-oz.) package chocolate
        wafer cookies
½   (4-oz.) semisweet chocolate
        baking bar, chopped
½   cup butter, melted
⅓   cup sugar

CHEESECAKE FILLING

1   (6-oz.) package white chocolate
        baking squares, chopped
¼   cup whipping cream
2   (8-oz.) packages cream cheese,
        softened
2   Tbsp. all-purpose flour
⅓   cup sugar
4   large eggs
½   cup chopped sweetened
        dried cranberries
½   (4-oz.) semisweet chocolate
        baking bar, finely chopped
¼   cup amaretto liqueur

1. Prepare Cranberry Topping: Bring first 2 ingredients and ¼ cup water to a boil in a 3-qt. saucepan over medium-high heat, stirring often. Boil, stirring often, 6 to 8 minutes or until mixture thickens to a syrup-like consistency. Remove from heat, and stir in jam. Cool completely (about 1 hour). Cover and chill 8 hours.

2. Prepare Piecrust: Preheat oven to 350°. Pulse wafer cookies and chopped semisweet chocolate in a food processor 8 to 10 times or until mixture resembles fine crumbs. Stir together crumb mixture, melted butter, and ⅓ cup sugar; firmly press on bottom, up sides, and onto lip of a lightly greased 10-inch pie plate. Bake 10 minutes. Transfer to a wire rack, and cool completely (about 30 minutes). Reduce oven temperature to 325°.

3. Prepare Cheesecake Filling: Microwave white chocolate and whipping cream at MEDIUM (50% power) 1 to 1½ minutes or until melted and smooth, stirring at 30-second intervals.

4. Beat cream cheese, flour, and ⅓ cup sugar at medium speed with an electric mixer 1 minute or until creamy and smooth. Add eggs, 1 at a time, beating just until blended after each addition. Add cranberries, next 2 ingredients, and white chocolate mixture. Beat at low speed just until blended. Spoon batter into prepared crust.

5. Bake at 325° for 30 to 35 minutes or until set. Cool completely on a wire rack (about 2 hours). Cover and chill 8 hours. Spoon topping over cheesecake before serving.

PUMPKIN-PECAN CHEESECAKE

MAKES: 12 servings ▪ **HANDS-ON TIME:** 25 min.
TOTAL TIME: 11 hours, 32 min., including Praline Topping and Pie-Glazed Pecans

2   cups graham cracker crumbs
⅓   cup finely chopped pecans
5   Tbsp. butter, melted
3   Tbsp. light brown sugar
4   (8-oz.) packages cream cheese,
        softened
1   cup granulated sugar
1   tsp. vanilla extract
4   large eggs
1½   cups canned pumpkin
1½   Tbsp. lemon juice
Praline Topping
Pie-Glazed Pecans
Garnish: fresh sage leaves

1. Preheat oven to 325°. Stir together first 4 ingredients in a bowl until well blended. Press mixture on bottom and 1½ inches up sides of a 9-inch springform pan. Bake 8 to 10 minutes or until lightly browned. Beat cream cheese and next 2 ingredients at medium speed with a heavy-duty electric stand mixer until blended and smooth. Add eggs, 1 at a time, beating just until blended after each addition. Add pumpkin and lemon juice, beating until blended. Pour batter into prepared crust. (Pan will be very full.)

2. Bake at 325° for 1 hour to 1 hour and 10 minutes or until almost set. Turn oven off. Let cheesecake stand in oven, with door closed, 15 minutes. Remove cheesecake from oven, and gently run a knife around outer edge of cheesecake to loosen from sides of pan. (Do not remove sides of pan.) Cool completely on a wire rack (about 1 hour). Cover and chill 8 to 24 hours. Remove sides and bottom of pan, and transfer cheesecake to a serving plate. Pour hot Praline Topping slowly over top of cheesecake, spreading to within ¼ inch of edge. Top with Pie-Glazed Pecans.

Praline Topping

MAKES: 1⅓ cups ▪ **HANDS-ON TIME:** 15 min. ▪ **TOTAL TIME:** 20 min.

1   cup firmly packed brown sugar
⅓   cup whipping cream
¼   cup butter
1   cup powdered sugar, sifted
1   tsp. vanilla extract

Bring first 3 ingredients to a boil in a 1-qt. saucepan over medium heat, stirring often. Boil, stirring occasionally, 1 minute; remove from heat. Gradually whisk in powdered sugar and vanilla until smooth. Let stand 5 minutes, whisking occasionally. Use immediately.

Pie-Glazed Pecans

MAKES: 2 cups ▪ **HANDS-ON TIME:** 15 min. ▪ **TOTAL TIME:** 35 min.

¼   cup dark corn syrup
2   Tbsp. sugar
2   cups pecan halves
Parchment paper

Preheat oven to 350°. Stir together dark corn syrup and sugar. Add pecans; stir until pecans are coated. Line a jelly-roll pan with parchment paper; coat parchment paper with cooking spray. Spread pecans in a single layer in prepared pan. Bake for 15 minutes or until glaze bubbles slowly and thickens, stirring every 3 minutes. Transfer pan to a wire rack. Spread pecans in a single layer, separating individual pecans; cool completely. Cooled pecans should be crisp; if not, bake 5 more minutes.

CRANBERRY-APPLE PIE WITH PECAN SHORTBREAD CRUST

MAKES: 12 servings ▪ **HANDS-ON TIME:** 30 min. ▪ **TOTAL TIME:** 3 hours, 30 min.

CRUST

1½ cups butter, softened
¾ cup powdered sugar
3 cups all-purpose flour
1 cup finely chopped toasted pecans

FILLING

3 lb. Gala apples
1 cup firmly packed light brown sugar
¾ cup sweetened dried cranberries
¼ cup all-purpose flour
1 tsp. ground cinnamon
2 Tbsp. butter, melted

Garnishes: toasted pecan halves, powdered sugar

1. Prepare Crust: Preheat oven to 350°. Beat butter at medium speed with an electric mixer 1 minute or until creamy; add powdered sugar, beating well. Gradually add flour, beating at low speed until mixture is no longer crumbly and starts to come together into a ball. Stir in toasted pecans. Shape one-third of dough into an 8-inch log; wrap in plastic wrap, and chill until ready to use. Press remaining dough on bottom and up sides of a 9-inch springform pan. Cover and chill crust.

2. Prepare Filling: Peel apples; cut into ¼-inch-thick wedges. Toss together apples and next 4 ingredients. Spoon mixture into prepared crust. Drizzle with melted butter.

3. Cut reserved dough log into 8 (1-inch) pieces. Gently shape each piece into a 6- to 8-inch rope. Lightly press each rope to flatten into strips. Arrange strips in a lattice design over filling.

4. Bake at 350° for 1 hour to 1 hour and 10 minutes or until juices are thick and bubbly, crust is golden brown, and apples are tender when pierced with a long wooden pick, shielding with foil during last 30 minutes to prevent excessive browning. Cool completely in pan on a wire rack. Remove sides of pan.

CHOCOLATE-PECAN CHESS PIE

MAKES: 8 servings ▪ **HANDS-ON TIME:** 15 min. ▪ **TOTAL TIME:** 2 hours, 5 min.

½ *(14.1-oz.) package refrigerated piecrusts*

½ *cup butter*

2 *(1-oz.) unsweetened chocolate baking squares*

1 *(5-oz.) can evaporated milk (⅔ cup)*

2 *large eggs*

2 *tsp. vanilla extract, divided*

1½ *cups granulated sugar*

3 *Tbsp. unsweetened cocoa*

2 *Tbsp. all-purpose flour*

⅛ *tsp. table salt*

1½ *cups pecan halves and pieces*

⅔ *cup firmly packed light brown sugar*

1 *Tbsp. light corn syrup*

1. Preheat oven to 350°. Roll piecrust into a 13-inch circle on a lightly floured surface. Fit into a 9-inch pie plate; fold edges under, and crimp.

2. Microwave butter and chocolate squares in a large microwave-safe bowl at MEDIUM (50% power) 1½ minutes or until melted and smooth, stirring at 30-second intervals. Whisk in evaporated milk, eggs, and 1 tsp. vanilla.

3. Stir together granulated sugar and next 3 ingredients. Add sugar mixture to chocolate mixture, whisking until smooth. Pour mixture into prepared crust.

4. Bake pie at 350° for 40 minutes. Stir together pecans, next 2 ingredients, and remaining 1 tsp. vanilla; sprinkle over pie. Bake 10 more minutes or until set. Remove from oven to a wire rack, and cool completely (about 1 hour).

Dark, rich, and intensely chocolaty, this is our favorite new twist on pecan pie. Make it even more special and serve with sweetened whipped cream.

BREAKFAST

Make the morning magical with egg casseroles, pancakes, and other favorites that everyone will love.

FRIED EGG
SANDWICHES

FRIED EGG SANDWICHES

MAKES: 4 servings ▪ **HANDS-ON TIME:** 25 min. ▪ **TOTAL TIME:** 27 min.

4   (½-inch-thick) challah bread
    slices
2   Tbsp. butter, melted
1   (0.9-oz.) envelope hollandaise
    sauce mix
¼   tsp. lemon zest
1½ tsp. fresh lemon juice, divided
2   cups loosely packed arugula
½   cup loosely packed fresh flat-leaf
    parsley leaves
¼   cup thinly sliced red onion
3   tsp. extra virgin olive oil, divided
4   large eggs
¼   tsp. kosher salt
¼   tsp. freshly ground black pepper
12 thin pancetta slices, cooked
2   Tbsp. chopped sun-dried
    tomatoes

1. Preheat broiler with oven rack 5 to 6 inches from heat. Brush both sides of bread with butter; place on an aluminum foil-lined broiler pan. Broil 1 to 2 minutes on each side or until lightly toasted.

2. Prepare hollandaise sauce according to package directions; stir in zest and ½ tsp. lemon juice. Keep warm.

3. Toss together arugula, parsley, onion, 2 tsp. olive oil, and remaining 1 tsp. lemon juice.

4. Heat remaining 1 tsp. olive oil in a large nonstick skillet over medium heat. Gently break eggs into hot skillet; sprinkle with salt and black pepper. Cook 2 to 3 minutes on each side or to desired degree of doneness.

5. Top bread slices with arugula mixture, pancetta slices, and fried eggs. Spoon hollandaise sauce over each egg, and sprinkle with tomatoes. Serve immediately.

SAUSAGE-EGG ROLLUPS

MAKES: 6 servings ▪ **HANDS-ON TIME:** 15 min. ▪ **TOTAL TIME:** 15 min.

½   lb. ground pork sausage
1   Tbsp. olive oil
5   large eggs
1   Tbsp. milk
Pinch of table salt
Pinch of black pepper
¾   cup (3 oz.) shredded sharp
    Cheddar cheese
½   cup salsa
6   (6-inch) fajita-size flour tortillas

1. Cook sausage in hot oil in a large nonstick skillet over medium-high heat 4 to 5 minutes or until browned; drain.

2. Whisk together eggs and next 3 ingredients in a large bowl.

3. Add egg mixture to skillet, and cook over medium-high heat, without stirring, 2 to 3 minutes or until eggs begin to set on bottom. Gently draw cooked edges away from sides of skillet to form large pieces. Cook, stirring occasionally, 4 to 5 minutes or until eggs are thickened and moist. (Do not overstir.)

4. Divide sausage, scrambled eggs, cheese, and salsa equally among tortillas, spooning ingredients down center of each tortilla. Roll up tortillas.

CREAMY EGG STRATA

MAKES: 8 to 10 servings ▪ **HANDS-ON TIME:** 35 min. ▪ **TOTAL TIME:** 10 hours, 10 min.

½ (16-oz.) French bread loaf, cubed
  (about 5 cups)
6 Tbsp. butter, divided
2 cups (8 oz.) shredded Swiss
  cheese
½ cup freshly grated Parmesan
  cheese
⅓ cup chopped onion
1 tsp. minced garlic
3 Tbsp. all-purpose flour
1½ cups chicken broth
¾ cup dry white wine
½ tsp. table salt
½ tsp. freshly ground black pepper
¼ tsp. ground nutmeg
½ cup sour cream
8 large eggs, lightly beaten
Garnish: chopped fresh chives

1. Place bread cubes in a well-buttered 13- x 9-inch baking dish. Melt 3 Tbsp. butter, and drizzle over bread cubes. Sprinkle with cheeses.

2. Melt remaining 3 Tbsp. butter in a medium saucepan over medium heat; add onion and garlic. Sauté 2 to 3 minutes or until tender. Whisk in flour until smooth; cook, whisking constantly, 2 to 3 minutes or until lightly browned. Whisk in broth and next 4 ingredients until blended. Bring mixture to a boil; reduce heat to medium-low, and simmer, stirring occasionally, 15 minutes or until thickened. Remove from heat. Stir in sour cream. Add additional salt and pepper to taste.

3. Gradually whisk about one-fourth of hot sour cream mixture into eggs; add egg mixture to remaining sour cream mixture, whisking constantly. Pour mixture over cheeses in baking dish. Cover with plastic wrap, and chill 8 to 24 hours.

4. Let strata stand at room temperature 1 hour. Preheat oven to 350°. Remove plastic wrap, and bake 30 minutes or until set. Serve immediately.

PLAN AHEAD

Prepare this recipe Christmas Eve morning and chill overnight so that all you have to do Christmas morning is put the casserole in the oven while you enjoy opening gifts with family.

CARAMELIZED ONION
QUICHE

CARAMELIZED ONION QUICHE

MAKES: 6 to 8 servings ▪ **HANDS-ON TIME:** 45 min. ▪ **TOTAL TIME:** 2 hours

1 (14.1-oz.) package refrigerated piecrusts
3 large sweet onions, sliced (about 1½ lb.)
2 Tbsp. olive oil
½ cup chopped fresh flat-leaf parsley
6 cooked bacon slices, crumbled
2 cups (8 oz.) shredded Gruyère cheese
1½ cups half-and-half
4 large eggs
½ tsp. table salt
¼ tsp. freshly ground black pepper
¼ tsp. ground nutmeg
Garnishes: additional chopped fresh parsley, chives, mint leaves

1. Preheat oven to 425°. Unroll piecrusts; stack on a lightly greased surface. Roll stacked piecrusts into a 12-inch circle. Fit piecrust into a 10-inch deep-dish tart pan with removable bottom; press into fluted edges. Trim off excess piecrust along edges. Line piecrust with aluminum foil and fill with pie weights or dried beans. Place pan on a foil-lined baking sheet. Bake 12 minutes. Remove weights and foil, and bake 8 more minutes. Cool completely on baking sheet on a wire rack (about 15 minutes). Reduce oven temperature to 350°.

2. Meanwhile, cook onions in hot oil in a large skillet over medium-high heat, stirring often, 15 to 20 minutes or until onions are caramel colored. Remove from heat, and stir in parsley and bacon. Place half of onion mixture in tart shell, and top with half of cheese; repeat with remaining onion mixture and cheese.

3. Whisk together half-and-half and next 4 ingredients; pour over cheese.

4. Bake at 350° for 40 to 45 minutes or until set. Cool on baking sheet on a wire rack 15 minutes before serving.

ASPARAGUS FRITTATA

MAKES: 6 servings ▪ **HANDS-ON TIME:** 30 min. ▪ **TOTAL TIME:** 30 min.

1 lb. fresh thin asparagus
2 Tbsp. butter
1 small onion, coarsely chopped
1 garlic clove, minced
12 large eggs
½ cup sour cream
¾ tsp. freshly ground black pepper
½ tsp. kosher salt
1 cup (4 oz.) shredded Gouda cheese
¼ cup freshly grated Parmesan cheese

1. Preheat oven to 350° with oven rack 6 inches from top of heat source. Cut asparagus diagonally into 1-inch pieces, discarding tough ends. Melt butter in a 10-inch ovenproof skillet over medium-high heat. Add onion; sauté 3 to 4 minutes or until tender. Add asparagus; sauté 3 to 4 minutes or until tender. Add garlic, and sauté 1 minute.

2. Whisk together eggs and next 3 ingredients until well blended. Stir in ¾ cup Gouda cheese. Fold egg mixture into vegetable mixture in skillet. Cook, stirring occasionally, 2 to 3 minutes or until almost set. Sprinkle with Parmesan cheese and remaining ¼ cup Gouda cheese.

3. Bake at 350° for 5 minutes or until set. Increase oven temperature to broil, and broil 3 to 4 minutes or until golden brown.

GRITS-AND-GREENS BREAKFAST BAKE

Give yourself a head start: Make Simple Collard Greens up to three days ahead.

MAKES: 8 servings ▪ **HANDS-ON TIME:** 25 min. ▪ **TOTAL TIME:** 2 hours, 7 min., including collard greens

1   tsp. table salt
1½   cups uncooked quick-cooking
     grits
1   cup (4 oz.) shredded white
     Cheddar cheese
3   Tbsp. butter
½   cup half-and-half
¼   tsp. freshly ground black pepper
¼   tsp. ground red pepper
2   large eggs
3   cups Simple Collard Greens,
     drained
8   large eggs
Hot sauce (optional)

1. Preheat oven to 375°. Bring table salt and 4 cups water to a boil in a large saucepan over medium-high heat; gradually whisk in grits. Reduce heat to medium, and cook, whisking often, 5 to 7 minutes or until thickened. Remove from heat, and stir in cheese and butter.

2. Whisk together half-and-half, black pepper, red pepper, and 2 eggs in a medium bowl. Stir half-and-half mixture into grits mixture. Stir in Simple Collard Greens. Pour mixture into a lightly greased 13- x 9-inch baking dish.

3. Bake at 375° for 25 to 30 minutes or until set. Remove from oven.

4. Make 8 indentations in grits mixture with back of a large spoon. Break remaining 8 eggs, 1 at a time, and slip 1 egg into each indentation. Bake at 375° for 12 to 14 minutes or until eggs are cooked to desired degree of doneness. Cover loosely with aluminum foil, and let stand 10 minutes. Serve with hot sauce, if desired.

Simple Collard Greens

MAKES: 3 cups ▪ **HANDS-ON TIME:** 10 min. ▪ **TOTAL TIME:** 50 min.

½   medium-size sweet onion,
     chopped
2   Tbsp. olive oil
1   (16-oz.) package fresh collard
     greens, washed, trimmed,
     and chopped
1½   tsp. table salt

Cook onion in hot oil in a large Dutch oven over medium heat, stirring occasionally, 10 minutes or until tender. Add collard greens, salt, and 3 cups water. Bring to a boil; reduce heat, and simmer 30 minutes or until tender.

SLOW-COOKER GRITS

Simplify your morning: Soak the grits the night before.

MAKES: 8 servings ▪ **HANDS-ON TIME:** 10 min. ▪ **TOTAL TIME:** 10 hours, 10 min.

2 cups uncooked stone-ground grits
¼ cup heavy cream
2 Tbsp. butter
1½ tsp. table salt
½ tsp. black pepper
Toppings: boiled shrimp, shredded Cheddar cheese, sliced smoked sausage, chopped green onion, chopped chives

1. Stir together grits and 6 cups water in a 5- or 6-qt. slow cooker. Let stand 1 to 2 minutes, allowing grits to settle to bottom. Tilt cooker slightly; skim off solids using a fine wire-mesh strainer. Cover; soak 8 hours or overnight.
2. Cover and cook grits on HIGH 2 hours to 2 hours and 30 minutes, stirring halfway through. Stir in cream and next 3 ingredients. Serve with desired toppings.

Create a Grits Bar

Offer these toppings with a few staples.

Bourbon Mushrooms: Melt ¼ cup butter with ¼ cup olive oil in a large skillet over medium heat; add 2 lb. sliced assorted fresh mushrooms, ¾ tsp. salt, and ¼ tsp. black pepper. Cook, stirring occasionally, 12 to 15 minutes or until tender and almost all liquid has evaporated. Remove from heat. Stir in ½ cup bourbon or chicken broth; return to heat, and cook 2 to 3 minutes or until slightly thickened. Reduce heat to low; stir in 3 garlic cloves, minced; 2 Tbsp. chopped fresh parsley; and 1 Tbsp. chopped fresh thyme. Cook 1 more minute. Makes: 8 to 10 servings.

Easy Creole Sauce: Sauté 2 celery ribs, chopped, in 2 Tbsp. olive oil in a saucepan over medium heat 3 to 4 minutes until tender. Stir in 2 (14.5-oz.) cans diced tomatoes with green peppers and onion; 3 garlic cloves, minced; 2 tsp. Creole seasoning; and 1 tsp. sugar. Reduce heat to low; simmer, stirring occasionally, 20 minutes. Stir in 2 Tbsp. chopped fresh flat-leaf parsley; 2 green onions, thinly sliced; and 1 tsp. hot sauce. Store in refrigerator up to 2 days. Makes: 3 cups.

Great Grits Combos
Boiled Shrimp + Easy Creole Sauce
Bourbon Mushrooms + Spinach + Swiss + Bacon
Chopped Ham + Shredded Cheddar
Caramelized Onions + Shredded Smoked Gruyère
Shredded Barbecued Pork + BBQ Sauce + Sautéed Spinach

MINI GRITS AND GREENS

Warm ceramic soup spoons in a 200° oven for 10 minutes before assembling.

MAKES: 3 dozen ▪ **HANDS-ON TIME:** 25 min. ▪ **TOTAL TIME:** 45 min.

1 cup chicken broth
⅓ cup half-and-half
¼ tsp. table salt
½ cup uncooked regular grits
½ cup (2 oz.) freshly shredded
    Cheddar cheese
¼ cup freshly grated Parmesan
    cheese
1 Tbsp. butter
½ tsp. hot sauce
¼ tsp. freshly ground black pepper
8 large fresh collard green leaves
2 small dry Spanish chorizo
    sausage links (about 2¾ oz.)
1 Tbsp. olive oil
2 tsp. apple cider vinegar
½ tsp. sugar
36 porcelain tasting spoons,
    warmed
Garnish: chopped fresh chives

1. Bring first 3 ingredients and 1 cup water to a boil in a medium saucepan over high heat; gradually whisk in grits. Cover, reduce heat to medium-low, and simmer, stirring occasionally, 15 minutes or until thickened. Whisk in Cheddar cheese and next 4 ingredients, whisking constantly until cheese melts. Keep warm.

2. Rinse collard greens. Trim and discard thick stems from bottom of collard green leaves (about 2 inches). Stack collard greens on a cutting board. Tightly roll up leaves, and thinly slice into ⅛-inch strips. Quarter chorizo lengthwise, and cut into small pieces.

3. Sauté chorizo in hot oil in a large skillet over medium-high heat 2 minutes. Add collard greens, vinegar, and sugar. Cook, stirring constantly, 2 minutes or until greens are bright green and just tender. Add additional salt and pepper to taste.

4. Place about 1 Tbsp. grits onto each warm spoon, and top with collard mixture. Serve immediately.

Note: We tested with Quijote Chorizos Caseros Home-Style Dry Sausage.

CRACKER SPOONS
with Pimiento Cheese

MAKES: 5 dozen ▪ **HANDS-ON TIME:** 25 min. ▪ **TOTAL TIME:** 1 hour, 10 min.

1½ (14.1-oz.) packages refrigerated
    piecrusts
1 large egg white, beaten
¾ tsp. seasoned salt
Parchment paper
Homemade or store-bought
    pimiento cheese
Garnishes: diced pimiento,
    chopped fresh chives

1. Preheat oven to 400°. Unroll piecrusts; brush with egg white, and sprinkle with seasoned salt (about ¼ tsp. per crust). Cut dough into shapes using a 4½- or 5-inch teaspoon-shaped cutter. Place cutouts 1 inch apart on parchment paper-lined baking sheets.

2. Bake, in batches, at 400° for 9 to 11 minutes or until lightly browned and crisp. Remove from baking sheets to a wire rack, and cool completely (about 20 minutes). Store in an airtight container 1 day, or freeze up to 2 weeks.

3. Spoon pimiento cheese into a zip-top plastic freezer bag. (Do not seal.) Snip 1 corner of bag to make a small hole. Pipe pimiento cheese onto end of each spoon.

MINI GRITS AND GREENS

CRACKER SPOONS WITH
PIMIENTO CHEESE

GEORGIA GRITS WAFFLES

MAKES: 8 servings ▪ **HANDS-ON TIME:** 25 min. ▪ **TOTAL TIME:** 50 min., not including toppings

½ cup uncooked regular grits
6 Tbsp. cold unsalted butter, cubed
2 large eggs, lightly beaten
¾ cup buttermilk
1¼ cups all-purpose flour
1 Tbsp. sugar
2 tsp. baking powder
½ tsp. baking soda
Toppings: Vanilla Crème Anglaise (optional), Maple-Bacon Praline Syrup (optional)

1. Bring 2 cups water to a boil over medium-high heat in a medium saucepan. Whisk in grits; bring to a boil. Reduce heat to low; cook, stirring often, 15 minutes or until tender. Stir in butter until melted; cool to room temperature. Stir in eggs and buttermilk.
2. Whisk together flour and next 3 ingredients in a small bowl. Stir flour mixture into grits mixture until just combined.
3. Cook in a preheated, oiled waffle iron until golden (about ⅓ cup batter each). Remove from iron. Serve with Vanilla Crème Anglaise and Maple-Bacon Praline Syrup, if desired.

Vanilla Crème Anglaise

MAKES: 1 cup ▪ **HANDS-ON TIME:** 20 min. ▪ **TOTAL TIME:** 20 min.

½ cup 2% reduced-fat milk
½ cup heavy cream
3 large egg yolks
¼ cup sugar
Pinch of kosher salt
½ tsp. vanilla extract

1. Heat milk and cream in a heavy saucepan over medium-low heat just until bubbles and steam appear (do not boil).
2. Reduce heat to low. Whisk together egg yolks and next 2 ingredients in a bowl; gradually whisk in one-fourth of hot milk mixture. Gradually add warm egg mixture to remaining hot milk mixture, whisking constantly; cook, whisking constantly, 7 minutes or until mixture thinly coats the back of a wooden spoon. Remove from heat. Whisk in vanilla.
3. Pour through a fine wire-mesh strainer into a large bowl. Serve warm.

Maple-Bacon Praline Syrup

MAKES: about 1 cup ▪ **HANDS-ON TIME:** 5 min. ▪ **TOTAL TIME:** 5 min.

½ cup butter
½ cup chopped pecans
½ cup pure maple syrup
2 thick hickory-smoked bacon slices, cooked and crumbled

Cook all ingredients in a saucepan over medium-low heat, stirring often, 5 minutes or until blended.

ITALIAN CREAM PANCAKES

MAKES: about 18 pancakes ▪ HANDS-ON TIME: 35 min. ▪ TOTAL TIME: 50 min., including syrup

2 cups all-purpose flour
⅓ cup sugar
1 tsp. baking powder
½ tsp. baking soda
½ tsp. table salt
1 cup buttermilk
¾ cup heavy cream
2 Tbsp. butter, melted
2 tsp. vanilla extract
2 large eggs, separated
⅔ cup finely chopped toasted pecans
½ cup sweetened flaked coconut
Cream Cheese Syrup
Garnish: chopped toasted pecans

1. Stir together flour and next 4 ingredients in a large bowl. Whisk together buttermilk, next 3 ingredients, and 2 egg yolks in another bowl. Gradually stir buttermilk mixture into flour mixture just until dry ingredients are moistened. Stir in toasted pecans and coconut. Beat egg whites at high speed with an electric mixer until stiff peaks form; fold into batter.

2. Pour about ¼ cup batter for each pancake onto a hot, buttered griddle or large nonstick skillet. Cook pancakes over medium heat 3 to 4 minutes or until tops are covered with bubbles and edges look dry and cooked. Turn and cook 3 to 4 minutes or until done. (Keep pancakes warm in a 200° oven up to 30 minutes.) Stack pancakes on individual plates. Serve with Cream Cheese Syrup.

Cream Cheese Syrup

MAKES: 1¼ cups ▪ HANDS-ON TIME: 10 min. ▪ TOTAL TIME: 10 min.

½ (8-oz.) package cream cheese, softened
¼ cup butter, softened
¼ cup maple syrup
1 tsp. vanilla extract
1 cup powdered sugar
¼ cup milk

Beat first 4 ingredients at medium speed with an electric mixer until creamy. Gradually add sugar, beating until smooth. Gradually add milk, beating until smooth. If desired, microwave in a microwave-safe bowl at HIGH 10 to 15 seconds or just until warm; stir until smooth.

GERMAN CHOCOLATE PANCAKES

MAKES: about 20 pancakes ▪ HANDS-ON TIME: 35 min. ▪ TOTAL TIME: 55 min., including syrup

2   cups all-purpose flour
½   cup sugar
½   cup unsweetened cocoa
1½   Tbsp. baking powder
1   tsp. table salt
2   cups milk
2   large eggs, lightly beaten
½   (4-oz.) sweet chocolate baking
     bar, finely chopped
3   Tbsp. butter, melted
1   tsp. vanilla extract
German Chocolate Syrup
Garnishes: chocolate curls, white
     chocolate curls

1. Whisk together first 5 ingredients in a large bowl. Whisk together milk and next 4 ingredients in another bowl. Gradually stir milk mixture into flour mixture just until moistened.

2. Pour about ¼ cup batter for each pancake onto a hot, buttered griddle or large nonstick skillet. Cook pancakes over medium heat 3 to 4 minutes or until tops are covered with bubbles and edges look dry and cooked. Turn and cook 3 to 4 minutes or until done. (Keep pancakes warm in a 200° oven up to 30 minutes.) Stack pancakes on individual plates. Serve with German Chocolate Syrup.

German Chocolate Syrup

MAKES: 1½ cups ▪ HANDS-ON TIME: 15 min. ▪ TOTAL TIME: 20 min.

⅔   cup chopped pecans
⅔   cup sweetened flaked coconut
1   (5-oz.) can evaporated milk
2   large egg yolks, lightly beaten
½   cup firmly packed light brown
     sugar
¼   cup butter, melted
½   tsp. vanilla extract

1. Preheat oven to 350°. Bake pecans and coconut in a single layer in a shallow pan 5 to 7 minutes or until lightly toasted and fragrant, stirring halfway through.

2. Cook evaporated milk and next 3 ingredients in a heavy 2-qt. saucepan over medium heat, stirring constantly, 8 to 10 minutes or until mixture bubbles and begins to thicken. Remove from heat, and stir in vanilla, pecans, and coconut. Serve immediately, or store in an airtight container in refrigerator up to 1 week.

Tip: To reheat, microwave syrup in a microwave-safe bowl at HIGH 10 to 15 seconds or just until warm; stir until smooth.

CREAM CHEESE-FILLED WREATH

MAKES: 10 to 12 servings ▪ **HANDS-ON TIME:** 30 min. ▪ **TOTAL TIME:** 10 hours, 15 min., including filling and glaze

1 (8-oz.) container sour cream
½ cup sugar
½ cup butter, cut up
1 tsp. table salt
2 (¼-oz.) envelopes active dry yeast
½ cup warm water (105° to 115°)
2 tsp. sugar
2 large eggs, lightly beaten
4 cups bread flour
Cream Cheese Filling
Vanilla Glaze
Garnish: sparkling sugar

1. Cook first 4 ingredients in a small saucepan over medium-low heat, stirring occasionally, 5 minutes or until butter melts. Cool until an instant-read thermometer registers 105° to 115° (about 10 minutes).

2. Combine yeast, warm water, and 2 tsp. sugar in a large bowl; let stand 5 minutes. Stir in sour cream mixture and eggs; gradually stir in flour. (Dough will be soft.) Cover and chill 8 to 24 hours.

3. Turn dough out onto a well-floured surface; knead 4 or 5 times. Roll dough into a 24- x 8-inch rectangle; spread with Cream Cheese Filling, leaving a 1-inch border around edges. Roll up dough, jelly-roll fashion, starting at 1 long side; press seam. Place, seam side down, on a lightly greased baking sheet. Bring ends of roll together to form a ring; moisten and pinch edges to seal. Cover; let rise in a warm place (80° to 85°), free from drafts, 1 hour or until doubled in bulk.

4. Preheat oven to 375°. Bake 20 to 22 minutes or until browned. Transfer to a serving plate. Drizzle with Vanilla Glaze.

Cream Cheese Filling

MAKES: 2 cups ▪ **HANDS-ON TIME:** 5 min. ▪ **TOTAL TIME:** 5 min.

2 (8-oz.) packages cream cheese, softened
½ cup sugar
1 large egg
2 tsp. vanilla extract

Beat all ingredients at medium speed with an electric mixer until smooth.

Vanilla Glaze

MAKES: about 1 cup ▪ **HANDS-ON TIME:** 5 min. ▪ **TOTAL TIME:** 5 min.

2½ cups powdered sugar
¼ cup milk
2 tsp. vanilla extract

Stir together all ingredients in a small bowl until blended.

OVERNIGHT COFFEE CRUMBLE CAKE

MAKES: 8 to 10 servings ▪ **HANDS-ON TIME:** 20 min. ▪ **TOTAL TIME:** 9 hours, 7 min., including crumble and drizzle

¾ cup butter, softened
1 cup sugar
2 large eggs
2 cups all-purpose flour
1 tsp. baking powder
1 tsp. baking soda
½ tsp. table salt
1 cup buttermilk
1 tsp. vanilla extract
Cinnamon-Nut Crumble
Sweet Bourbon Drizzle

1. Beat butter at medium speed with an electric mixer until creamy; gradually add sugar, beating well. Add eggs, 1 at a time, beating just until blended after each addition.

2. Combine flour and next 3 ingredients in a medium bowl. Add flour mixture to butter mixture alternately with buttermilk, beginning and ending with flour mixture. Stir in vanilla. Pour batter into a greased and floured 13- x 9-inch pan. Cover tightly, and chill 8 to 24 hours.

3. Preheat oven to 350°. Let cake stand at room temperature 30 minutes. Sprinkle with Cinnamon-Nut Crumble. Bake 32 to 35 minutes or until a wooden pick inserted in center comes out clean. Transfer to a serving plate; drizzle with Sweet Bourbon Drizzle.

Cinnamon-Nut Crumble

MAKES: 2 cups ▪ **HANDS-ON TIME:** 10 min. ▪ **TOTAL TIME:** 10 min.

½ cup coarsely chopped pecans
½ cup coarsely chopped walnuts
½ cup slivered almonds
½ cup firmly packed brown sugar
6 Tbsp. all-purpose flour
3 Tbsp. butter, melted
1 tsp. ground cinnamon

Stir together all ingredients in a medium bowl.

Sweet Bourbon Drizzle

MAKES: 1 cup ▪ **HANDS-ON TIME:** 5 min. ▪ **TOTAL TIME:** 5 min.

2 cups powdered sugar
1 Tbsp. bourbon
2 to 3 Tbsp. milk

Stir together powdered sugar, bourbon, and 2 Tbsp. milk in a small bowl. Stir in remaining 1 Tbsp. milk, 1 tsp. at a time, until desired consistency. Use immediately.

SWEET POTATO COFFEE CAKE

MAKES: 10 to 12 servings ▪ **HANDS-ON TIME:** 30 min. ▪ **TOTAL TIME:** 3 hours, including glaze

2 (¼-oz.) envelopes active dry yeast
½ cup warm water (105° to 115°)
1 tsp. granulated sugar
5½ cups bread flour, divided
1½ tsp. table salt
1 tsp. baking soda
1 cup cooked mashed sweet potato
1 large egg, lightly beaten
1 cup buttermilk
½ cup granulated sugar
¼ cup butter, melted
1 Tbsp. orange zest
⅔ cup granulated sugar
⅔ cup firmly packed brown sugar
1 Tbsp. ground cinnamon
¼ cup butter, melted
Caramel Glaze

1. Stir together first 3 ingredients in a 1-cup glass measuring cup; let stand 5 minutes.

2. Stir together 4½ cups bread flour, salt, and baking soda.

3. Beat yeast mixture and ½ cup bread flour at medium speed with a heavy-duty electric stand mixer until well blended. Gradually add sweet potato, next 5 ingredients, and flour mixture, beating until well blended.

4. Turn dough out onto a well-floured surface, and knead until smooth and elastic (about 4 to 5 minutes), gradually adding remaining ½ cup bread flour. Place dough in a lightly greased large bowl, turning to grease top. Cover and let rise in a warm place (80° to 85°), free from drafts, 1 to 1½ hours or until doubled in bulk.

5. Stir together ⅔ cup granulated sugar, brown sugar, and cinnamon. Punch dough down; turn out onto a well-floured surface. Divide dough in half. Roll 1 portion into a 16- x 12-inch rectangle. Brush with half of ¼ cup melted butter. Sprinkle with half of sugar mixture. Cut dough lengthwise into 6 (2-inch-wide) strips using a pizza cutter or knife.

6. Loosely coil 1 strip, and place in center of a lightly greased 10-inch round pan. Loosely coil remaining dough strips, 1 at a time, around center strip, attaching each to the end of the previous strip to make a single large spiral. (Sugared sides of dough strips should face center of spiral.) Repeat with remaining dough half, butter, and sugar mixture.

7. Cover; let rise in a warm place (80° to 85°), free from drafts, 30 minutes or until doubled in bulk.

8. Preheat oven to 350°. Bake 30 minutes or until lightly browned and a wooden pick inserted in center comes out clean. Cool in pans on a wire rack 10 minutes. Remove from pans to serving plates. Prepare Caramel Glaze, and brush over swirls.

Caramel Glaze

MAKES: 1½ cups ▪ **HANDS-ON TIME:** 15 min. ▪ **TOTAL TIME:** 15 min.

1 cup firmly packed brown sugar
½ cup butter
¼ cup evaporated milk
1 cup powdered sugar, sifted
1 tsp. vanilla extract

Bring first 3 ingredients to a boil in a 2-qt. saucepan over medium heat, whisking constantly. Boil, whisking constantly, 1 minute. Remove from heat; whisk in powdered sugar and vanilla until smooth. Stir gently 3 to 5 minutes or until mixture begins to cool and slightly thickens. Use immediately.

LEMON-ROSEMARY COFFEE CAKE

MAKES: 8 to 10 servings ▪ **HANDS-ON TIME:** 25 min. ▪ **TOTAL TIME:** 2 hours, 20 min.

Parchment paper
3   large lemons
2   cups all-purpose flour
1¼ cups sugar
½   tsp. table salt
½   cup very cold butter, cubed
1   tsp. baking powder
½   tsp. baking soda
¾   cup buttermilk*
1   large egg
1½ tsp. chopped fresh rosemary
1   (10-oz.) jar lemon curd
Powdered sugar
Garnishes: fresh rosemary sprigs,
      lemon slices, lemon rind curls

1. Preheat oven to 350°. Lightly grease bottom and sides of a 9-inch springform pan**. Line bottom of pan with parchment paper.

2. Grate zest from lemons to equal 1 Tbsp. Cut lemons in half; squeeze juice from lemons into a bowl to equal 5 Tbsp. Reserve zest and 1 Tbsp. lemon juice.

3. Pulse flour, sugar, and salt in a food processor 3 or 4 times or until blended. Add butter; pulse 6 or 7 times or until mixture resembles coarse crumbs. Reserve 1 cup flour mixture.

4. Transfer remaining flour mixture to bowl of a heavy-duty electric stand mixer. Add baking powder and baking soda; beat at low speed until well blended. Add buttermilk, egg, and ¼ cup lemon juice; beat at medium speed 1½ to 2 minutes or until batter is thoroughly blended, stopping to scrape bowl as needed. Stir in rosemary. Spoon half of batter into prepared pan.

5. Whisk lemon curd in a small bowl about 1 minute or until loosened and smooth; carefully spread over batter in pan. Top with remaining half of batter.

6. Stir together reserved lemon zest, 1 Tbsp. lemon juice, and 1 cup flour mixture; sprinkle lemon zest mixture over batter in pan.

7. Bake at 350° for 45 to 50 minutes or until a long wooden pick inserted in center comes out clean.

8. Cool in pan on a wire rack 10 minutes. Gently run a sharp knife around edge of cake to loosen; remove sides of pan. Cool cake completely on wire rack (about 1 hour). Dust with powdered sugar just before serving.

*Greek yogurt may be substituted.
**A 9-inch round cake pan may be substituted for springform pan. Line bottom and sides of cake pan with aluminum foil, allowing 2 to 3 inches to extend over sides; grease foil well. Proceed with recipe as directed through Step 7. Cool in pan on a wire rack 10 minutes. Lift cake from pan, using foil sides as handles. Carefully remove foil. Cool; dust with powdered sugar as directed.

MINI BANANA-CRANBERRY-NUT BREAD LOAVES

Use bananas that appear to be past their prime for this recipe.

MAKES: 5 miniature loaves ▪ **HANDS-ON TIME:** 20 min. ▪ **TOTAL TIME:** 1 hour, 25 min., including glaze

1   (8-oz.) package cream cheese, softened
¾   cup butter, softened
2   cups sugar
2   large eggs
3   cups all-purpose flour
½   tsp. baking powder
½   tsp. baking soda
½   tsp. table salt
1½ cups mashed ripe bananas
¾   cup chopped fresh cranberries
½   tsp. vanilla extract
¾   cup chopped toasted pecans
Orange Glaze

1. Preheat oven to 350°. Beat cream cheese and butter at medium speed with an electric mixer until creamy. Gradually add sugar, beating until light and fluffy. Add eggs, 1 at a time, beating just until blended after each addition.

2. Combine flour and next 3 ingredients; gradually add to butter mixture, beating at low speed just until blended. Stir in bananas and next 3 ingredients. Spoon about 1½ cups batter into each of 5 greased and floured 5- x 3-inch miniature loaf pans.

3. Bake at 350° for 40 to 44 minutes or until a wooden pick inserted in center comes out clean and sides pull away from pans. Cool in pans 10 minutes. Transfer to wire racks. Drizzle Orange Glaze over warm bread loaves, and cool 10 minutes.

Make Ahead: *Freeze baked, unglazed loaves in zip-top plastic freezer bags. Thaw loaves at room temperature. Reheat loaves at 300° for 10 to 12 minutes. Drizzle with glaze.*

Orange Glaze

MAKES: ½ cup ▪ **HANDS-ON TIME:** 5 min. ▪ **TOTAL TIME:** 5 min.

1   cup powdered sugar
1   tsp. orange zest
2 to 3 Tbsp. fresh orange juice

Stir together all ingredients in a small bowl until blended. Use immediately.

BLUEBERRY MUFFINS

MAKES: 1½ dozen ▪ **HANDS-ON TIME:** 15 min. ▪ **TOTAL TIME:** 40 min.

3½ cups all-purpose flour

1   cup sugar

1   Tbsp. baking powder

1½ tsp. table salt

3   large eggs

1½ cups milk

½ cup butter, melted

2   cups frozen blueberries

1   Tbsp. all-purpose flour

Lemon-Cream Cheese Glaze
  (optional)

Garnish: lemon zest

1. Preheat oven to 450°. Stir together first 4 ingredients. Whisk together eggs and next 2 ingredients; add to flour mixture, stirring just until dry ingredients are moistened. Toss blueberries with 1 Tbsp. flour, and gently fold into batter. Spoon mixture into 1½ lightly greased 12-cup muffin pans, filling three-fourths full.

2. Bake at 450° for 14 to 15 minutes or until lightly browned and a wooden pick inserted into center comes out clean. Immediately remove from pans to wire racks, and cool 10 minutes.

3. Meanwhile, prepare Lemon-Cream Cheese Glaze, and drizzle over warm muffins, if desired.

Fresh blueberries may be substituted for frozen blueberries.

Lemon-Cream Cheese Glaze

MAKES: ¾ cup ▪ **HANDS-ON TIME:** 10 min. ▪ **TOTAL TIME:** 10 min.

1   (3-oz.) package cream cheese,
  softened

1   tsp. lemon zest

1   Tbsp. fresh lemon juice

¼ tsp. vanilla extract

1½ cups sifted powdered sugar

Beat cream cheese at medium speed with an electric mixer until creamy. Add lemon zest, lemon juice, and vanilla; beat until smooth. Gradually add powdered sugar, beating until smooth.

OKRA-SHRIMP BEIGNETS

We took two Lowcountry favorites, okra and shrimp, and fried them into fritters that have the crispy and airy qualities of a good beignet, hence the name.

MAKES: about 30 ▪ **HANDS-ON TIME:** 27 min. ▪ **TOTAL TIME:** 47 min., including salsa and sour cream

Peanut oil
2   cups sliced fresh okra
½   green bell pepper, diced
½   medium onion, diced
1   large egg
½   cup all-purpose flour
¼   cup heavy cream
1   jalapeño pepper, finely chopped
¾   tsp. salt
¼   tsp. freshly ground pepper
¼   lb. unpeeled, medium-size
     raw shrimp, peeled and
     coarsely chopped
Fresh Tomato Salsa
Cilantro Sour Cream

1. Pour oil to depth of 3 inches in a Dutch oven; heat to 350°.

2. Stir together okra and next 8 ingredients in a large bowl until well blended; stir in shrimp.

3. Drop batter by rounded tablespoonfuls into hot oil, and fry, in batches, 2 to 3 minutes on each side or until golden brown. Drain on a wire rack over paper towels. Serve with Fresh Tomato Salsa and Cilantro Sour Cream.

Fresh Tomato Salsa

MAKES: 4 servings ▪ **HANDS-ON TIME:** 15 min. ▪ **TOTAL TIME:** 15 min.

4   large plum tomatoes, seeded
     and chopped (about 2 cups)
¼   cup fresh cilantro, chopped
1   jalapeño pepper, seeded and
     finely diced
3   Tbsp. red onion, finely diced
2½ Tbsp. fresh lime juice
1   Tbsp. extra virgin olive oil

Stir together all ingredients. Add salt and pepper to taste.

Cilantro Sour Cream

MAKES: 1 cup ▪ **HANDS-ON TIME:** 5 min. ▪ **TOTAL TIME:** 5 min.

1   (8-oz.) container sour cream
¼   cup fresh cilantro, chopped
1   tsp. lime zest
1   tsp. fresh lime juice
Garnish: fresh cilantro

Stir together all ingredients. Add salt and pepper to taste.

GOUDA GRITS

GOUDA GRITS

MAKES: 8 servings ■ **HANDS-ON TIME:** 10 min. ■ **TOTAL TIME:** 30 min.

4   cups chicken broth
1   cup whipping cream
1   tsp. table salt
¼   tsp. freshly ground black pepper
2   cups uncooked quick-cooking
       grits
2   cups (8 oz.) shredded Gouda
       cheese
½   cup buttermilk
¼   cup butter
2   tsp. hot sauce
Garnishes: shredded Gouda
       cheese, chopped green
       onions, black pepper

Bring first 4 ingredients and 4 cups water to a boil in a Dutch oven over high heat; whisk in grits, reduce heat to medium-low, and simmer, stirring occasionally, 15 minutes or until thickened. Remove from heat, and stir in Gouda and next 3 ingredients.

SUNSHINE CITRUS PLATTER

MAKES: 8 servings ■ **HANDS-ON TIME:** 20 min. ■ **TOTAL TIME:** 1 hour, 20 min.

4   navel oranges
2   Ruby Red or Rio Star grapefruit
2   Tbsp. powdered sugar
Ground cinnamon

1. Peel oranges and grapefruit; cut into ½-inch-thick rounds. Cover and chill 1 to 24 hours.
2. Arrange fruit on a large platter. Sift powdered sugar over fruit; sprinkle with cinnamon. Serve immediately.

BROWN SUGAR-AND-CORNMEAL-CRUSTED BACON

For easy cleanup, line the jelly-roll pans with aluminum foil.

MAKES: 8 servings ▪ **HANDS-ON TIME:** 15 min. ▪ **TOTAL TIME:** 1 hour

¼ **cup plain yellow cornmeal**
3 **Tbsp. brown sugar**
1½ **tsp. freshly ground black pepper**
16 **thick bacon slices**

1. Preheat oven to 400°. Combine first 3 ingredients in a shallow dish. Dredge bacon slices in cornmeal mixture, shaking off excess.

2. Place half of bacon in a single layer on a lightly greased wire rack in a jelly-roll pan. Place remaining bacon in a single layer on another lightly greased wire rack in a second jelly-roll pan.

3. Bake at 400° for 25 to 30 minutes or until browned and crisp. Cool 5 minutes.

METRIC EQUIVALENTS

The recipes that appear in this cookbook use the standard United States method for measuring liquid and dry or solid ingredients (teaspoons, tablespoons, and cups). The information in the following charts is provided to help cooks outside the U.S. successfully use these recipes. All equivalents are approximate.

Metric Equivalents for Different Types of Ingredients

A standard cup measure of a dry or solid ingredient will vary in weight depending on the type of ingredient. A standard cup of liquid is the same volume for any type of liquid. Use the following chart when converting standard cup measures to grams (weight) or milliliters (volume).

Standard Cup	Fine Powder (ex. flour)	Grain (ex. rice)	Granular (ex. sugar)	Liquid Solids (ex. butter)	Liquid (ex. milk)
1	140 g	150 g	190 g	200 g	240 ml
¾	105 g	113 g	143 g	150 g	180 ml
⅔	93 g	100 g	125 g	133 g	160 ml
½	70 g	75 g	95 g	100 g	120 ml
⅓	47 g	50 g	63 g	67 g	80 ml
¼	35 g	38 g	48 g	50 g	60 ml
⅛	18 g	19 g	24 g	25 g	30 ml

Useful Equivalents for Dry Ingredients by Weight

(To convert ounces to grams, multiply the number of ounces by 30.)

1 oz	=	¹⁄₁₆ lb	=	30 g
4 oz	=	¼ lb	=	120 g
8 oz	=	½ lb	=	240 g
12 oz	=	¾ lb	=	360 g
16 oz	=	1 lb	=	480 g

Useful Equivalents for Length

(To convert inches to centimeters, multiply the number of inches by 2.5.)

1 in				=		2.5 cm	
6 in	=	½ ft		=		15 cm	
12 in	=	1 ft		=		30 cm	
36 in	=	3 ft	=	1 yd	=	90 cm	
40 in				=		100 cm	= 1 m

Useful Equivalents for Liquid Ingredients by Volume

¼ tsp						=	1 ml
½ tsp						=	2 ml
1 tsp						=	5 ml
3 tsp	=	1 Tbsp			½ fl oz	=	15 ml
		2 Tbsp	=	⅛ cup	1 fl oz	=	30 ml
		4 Tbsp	=	¼ cup	2 fl oz	=	60 ml
		5⅓ Tbsp	=	⅓ cup	3 fl oz	=	80 ml
		8 Tbsp	=	½ cup	4 fl oz	=	120 ml
		10⅔ Tbsp	=	⅔ cup	5 fl oz	=	160 ml
		12 Tbsp	=	¾ cup	6 fl oz	=	180 ml
		16 Tbsp	=	1 cup	8 fl oz	=	240 ml
		1 pt	=	2 cups	16 fl oz	=	480 ml
		1 qt	=	4 cups	32 fl oz	=	960 ml
					33 fl oz	=	1000 ml = 1 l

Useful Equivalents for Cooking/Oven Temperatures

	Fahrenheit	Celsius	Gas Mark
Freeze water	32° F	0° C	
Room temperature	68° F	20° C	
Boil water	212° F	100° C	
Bake	325° F	160° C	3
	350° F	180° C	4
	375° F	190° C	5
	400° F	200° C	6
	425° F	220° C	7
	450° F	230° C	8
Broil			Grill

INDEX

*Page numbers preceded by an **F** indicate the Flip Section.*

ISBN-13: 978-0-8487-4351-2
ISBN-10: 0-8487-4351-2

Printed in the United States of America
First Printing 2014

Oxmoor House

Editorial Director: Leah McLaughlin
Creative Director: Felicity Keane
Art Director: Christopher Rhoads
Executive Food Director: Grace Parisi
Senior Editor: Rebecca Brennan
Managing Editor: Elizabeth Tyler Austin
Assistant Managing Editor: Jeanne de Lathouder

Southern Living Christmas Cookbook and Year-Round Celebrations

Senior Designer: Melissa Clark
Assistant Test Kitchen Manager: Alyson Moreland Haynes
Recipe Testers and Developers: Tamara Goldis, R.D.;
    Stefanie Maloney; Callie Nash; Karen Rankin;
    Wendy Treadwell, R.D.; Leah Van Deren
Food Stylists: Victoria E. Cox, Margaret Monroe Dickey,
    Catherine Crowell Steele
Photography Director: Jim Bathie
Senior Photographer: Hélène Dujardin
Senior Photo Stylists: Kay E. Clarke, Mindi Shapiro Levine
Senior Production Managers: Greg A. Amason,
    Sue Chodakiewicz

Contributors

Editor: Elizabeth Laseter
Project Editor: Melissa Brown
Compositor: Carol Damsky
Copy Editor: Donna Baldone
Proofreader: Barry Wise Smith
Indexer: Mary Ann Laurens
Fellows: Ali Carruba, Kylie Dazzo, Anna Ramia,
    Deanna Sakal, April Smitherman, Megan Thompson,
    Tonya West, Amanda Widis
Photographer: Iain Bagwell
Photo Stylist: Caitlin Van Horn

Southern Living®

Editor: Sid Evans
Creative Director: Robert Perino
Managing Editor: Candace Higginbotham
Executive Editors: Hunter Lewis, Jessica S. Thuston
Deputy Food Director: Whitney Wright
Test Kitchen Director: Robby Melvin
Test Kitchen Specialist/Food Styling:
    Vanessa McNeil Rocchio
Test Kitchen Professional: Pam Lolley
Recipe Editor: JoAnn Weatherly
Style Director: Heather Chadduck Hillegas
Director of Photography: Jeanne Dozier Clayton
Photographers: Robbie Caponetto, Laurey W. Glenn,
    Hector Sanchez
Assistant Photo Editor: Kate Phillips Robertson
Photo Coordinator: Chris Ellenbogen
Senior Photo Stylist: Buffy Hargett Miller
Assistant Photo Stylist: Caroline M. Cunningham
Photo Administrative Assistant: Courtney Authement
Editorial Assistant: Pat York

Time Home Entertainment Inc.

President and Publisher: Jim Childs
Vice President and Associate Publisher: Margot Schupf
Vice President, Finance: Vandana Patel
Executive Director, Marketing Services: Carol Pittard
Publishing Director: Megan Pearlman
Assistant General Counsel: Simone Procas

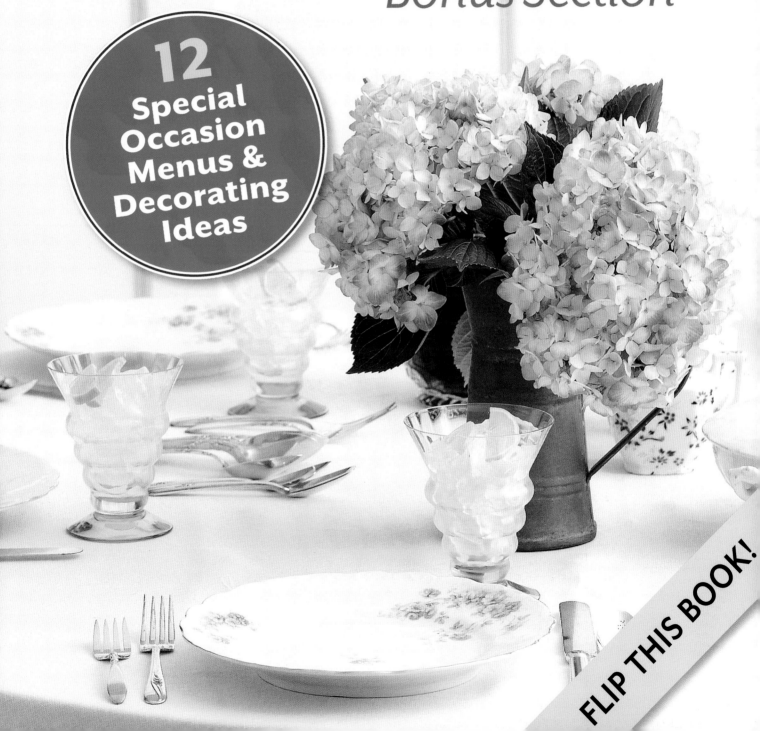

Southern Living

YEAR-ROUND CELEBRATIONS

Bonus Section

12 Special Occasion Menus & Decorating Ideas

FLIP THIS BOOK!

Dillard's Presents

Southern Living

YEAR-ROUND CELEBRATIONS

12 Special Occasion Menus & Decorating Ideas

CONTENTS

CELEBRATE YOUR FAVORITE YEAR-ROUND HOLIDAYS!

Christmas may be over, but the party doesn't have to end yet. On the following pages, you'll find 12 deliciously seasonal menus for holidays throughout the year, plus anytime special occasions such as bridal and baby showers. From great-tasting food to show-stopping table settings, each menu shows you simple ways to welcome guests. So whether you're throwing a spirited tailgating party or planning a laid-back summer picnic, the entertaining experts at Southern Living have you covered all year long.

SET A FESTIVE TABLE

Every great party comes together at an engaging table. From signature cocktails to personalized favors, these three settings are chock-full of easy ideas for making guests feel welcome at your next summer gathering.

GOLDEN GLOW

Capture the warmth of summer sun on your tabletop with staples in cheery hues and accessories that have a Midas touch.

1. Bring home the gold. Just as metallic accessories bring a certain level of on-trend finish to a summer outfit, the warm tones of brushed gold flatware and embellished glasses add finesse and sparkle to this casual table setting.

2. Get the conversation started. Finish off each place setting with playful icebreakers printed on colorful cardstock and mounted in vintage French flower frogs. Your guests will have a blast getting to know each other better.

3. Make your own to-go containers. Give guests a blooming party favor that mimics the lush centerpiece. These colorful vases are an easy DIY: Just dip julep cups into a can of mint green latex paint (while wearing a glove!), and let dry. Cardstock flags printed with names designate one for each of your guests.

4. Show off a personal collection. Set the table with a variety of glasses in different shapes and colors to create a more dynamic tableau—and to help guests keep track of their drinks. Shop eBay or Etsy for an eclectic mix of vintage styles, and garnish each with an antique cocktail stirrer.

Style Shortcut

Not every tablescape needs a load of linens. Here, the bare weathered-wood table lends textural contrast to the smooth, polished china and flatware. Round out the material mix with translucent accessories, such as glass jugs or Lucite napkin rings.

Style Shortcut

For an unexpected—and functional—centerpiece, stack cake stands topped with petits fours. Balance the dessert display's height with a collection of ceramic pitchers filled with round hydrangea and viburnum blooms.

CASUAL AFFAIR

Elevate your everyday routine by mixing pretty basics with personal touches for a simple spring table setting that's anything but mundane.

1. Dress down your drink station. A giant Mason jar-inspired container filled with pink lemonade is a casual alternative to the traditional punch bowl and a silver ladle helps make the setup special. Finish it off with lime slices for extra flavor.

2. Layer shapes and colors. Take a mix-and-match approach, combining plates and glasses of different hues and sizes within one place setting. Here, a colorful charger stands in for a place mat, and a vintage cocktail fork holds a handwritten place card.

3. Send guests home with a gift. Set out a tray of party favors for guests to pick up as they leave. A green-and-white-striped ribbon tied in a dapper bow gives these mini bottles of rosé a more festive feel.

4. Incorporate something vintage. Let an antique collection, like this set of butter plates, inspire the palette for your table. The dishes' delicate pattern enlivens the solid serving ware and ties together the colorful place setting.

TAILORED FIT

Take a cue from summer's signature light and airy fabric—seersucker— to create a table setting with a preppy twist on traditional Southern style.

1. Mix posh with plain. Footed sherbet dishes, ornate chargers and dessert plates, and sterling flatware pair with more casual pieces, such as simple white dinner plates, ink-jet printed menus, and grosgrain-trimmed cotton napkins, for a look that's high style but not at all fussy.

2. Add elegance with fresh flowers. Showcase the bounty of the season with a lush arrangement of pink peonies, white hydrangeas, and green viburnums. Presenting them in a silver punch bowl lends just the right level of refinement to the table.

3. Carry out your colors. Offer cheery drinks in green bottles that match the tablecloth, accented with pink monogrammed labels and straws that match your flowers. (Sprite bottles are the perfect hue.)

Dress the part by wearing seersucker clothing in similar shades.

4. Set up a self-serve bar. Set up a folding tray table that stands in for a bar so guests can help themselves to punch and nibbles like pimiento cheese and crackers. Take the tray outside to create an inviting spot for socializing before and after the meal.

Style Shortcut

The tablecloth's dressmaker details, such as its box-pleat skirt, are a nod to seersucker's traditional use in fashion. Layered toppers with scalloped edges add shapely pops of color.

YEAR-ROUND MENUS

From fresh spring flavors to vivid fall colors, our 12 seasonally inspired menus and table settings make for party-perfect entertaining throughout the entire year.

MENU

Glazed Spiral-Cut Ham

Spring Pea Orzo

Asparagus with Red Pepper Chowchow

Carrot-Ginger Puree

Hot Potato Salad

Easter-Egg Shortbread Cookies

EASTER CELEBRATION

Gather your family and friends around the table for a candy-colored Easter celebration with classic and modern elements. The place setting is simple, but details such as gold bands on the china and etching on the stemware say special occasion.

GLAZED SPIRAL-CUT HAM

HOT POTATO SALAD

SPRING PEA ORZO

CARROT-GINGER PUREE

ASPARAGUS WITH RED PEPPER CHOWCHOW

GLAZED SPIRAL-CUT HAM

We love a spiral-cut ham, but we don't like the sugary mystery glaze that comes with it. Use one of our three easy and unique glaze recipes instead.

MAKES: 8 TO 10 SERVINGS ■ **HANDS-ON TIME:** 10 MIN.
TOTAL TIME: 3 HOURS, 20 MIN., NOT INCLUDING GLAZES

1. Preheat oven to 350°. Place 1 (8- to 9-lb.) fully cooked, bone-in spiral-cut ham half, cut side down, in a heavy-duty aluminum foil-lined jelly-roll pan; let stand at room temperature 30 minutes.

2. Brush ½ cup desired glaze over ham. Bake, uncovered, on lowest oven rack 2 ½ to 3 hours or until a meat thermometer inserted into thickest portion registers 140°, basting every 30 minutes with ½ cup glaze.

3. Remove from oven, and spoon pan drippings over ham. Let stand 10 minutes.

Note: *We tested with Smithfield All Natural Spiral Sliced Smoked Uncured Ham.*

Pineapple-Prosecco Glaze

1¼ cups pineapple preserves
½ cup Prosecco or Cava
½ tsp. kosher salt

Pulse all ingredients in a food processor 6 or 7 times or until smooth. Makes 1½ cups.

Cola-Dijon-Brown Sugar Glaze

1½ cups firmly packed dark brown sugar
½ cup cola soft drink
½ cup Dijon mustard
½ tsp. kosher salt

Stir together all ingredients until smooth. Makes 1½ cups.

Coffee-and-Pepper Jelly Glaze

1¼ cups red pepper jelly
½ cup strong brewed coffee
½ tsp. kosher salt

Stir together all ingredients until well blended. Makes 1½ cups.

SPRING PEA ORZO

The key to this salad is to toss the warm pasta with the dressing so the orzo soaks up flavor.

MAKES: 6 SERVINGS ■ **HANDS-ON TIME:** 20 MIN.
TOTAL TIME: 1 HOUR, 30 MIN.

3   **to 4 lemons**
8   **oz. uncooked orzo pasta**
¼   **cup minced shallot or red onion**
2   **Tbsp. extra virgin olive oil**
1   **Tbsp. Dijon mustard**
½   **tsp. table salt**
½   **tsp. freshly ground black pepper**
1½ **cups cooked fresh or frozen peas**
1   **cup snow peas or sugar snap peas, blanched and chopped**
1   **cup assorted chopped fresh herbs (such as mint, chives, and parsley)**
½   **cup sliced almonds, toasted**

1. Grate zest from lemons to equal 2 tsp. loosely packed. Cut lemons in half; squeeze juice from lemons into a measuring cup to equal ½ cup.

2. Prepare pasta according to package directions. Whisk together shallots, next 4 ingredients, and lemon juice. Toss together pasta and shallot mixture. Cover with plastic wrap, and chill 1 to 48 hours.

3. Toss together pasta, peas, snow peas, next 2 ingredients, and lemon zest just before serving. Add salt, pepper, and additional lemon juice to taste.

A LUSH CENTERPIECE

In the center, a glass-footed compote lined with moss explodes with cabbage roses, sweet peas, tulips, and spray roses. Fern fronds and other bits of greenery add texture and balance, while glass bud vases filled with like blooms echo the theme down the table.

ASPARAGUS WITH RED PEPPER CHOWCHOW

Serve leftover chowchow with cheese and crackers, ham sandwiches, or burgers.

MAKES: 4 TO 6 SERVINGS ■ **HANDS-ON TIME:** 15 MIN.
TOTAL TIME: 15 MIN., NOT INCLUDING CHOWCHOW

1   *lb. fresh asparagus*
1   *(8-oz.) package fresh sugar snap peas, trimmed*
1   *(6-oz.) package fresh English peas*
1   *Tbsp. butter or olive oil*
2   *Tbsp. Red Pepper Chowchow*

1. Snap off and discard tough ends of asparagus. Blanch asparagus, and pat dry with paper towels. Repeat with sugar snap peas and English peas.
2. Melt butter in a large skillet over medium-high heat. Add asparagus, sugar snap peas, and English peas, and sauté 3 minutes or until thoroughly heated. Stir in Red Pepper Chowchow, and sauté 1 minute. Serve immediately.

Red Pepper Chowchow

MAKES: 1½ CUPS ■ **HANDS-ON TIME:** 20 MIN.
TOTAL TIME: 50 MIN.

3   *red bell peppers, chopped*
½   *medium-size sweet onion, chopped*
3   *garlic cloves, finely chopped*
⅓   *cup olive oil*
¼   *cup white wine vinegar*
1¼   *tsp. kosher salt*
½   *tsp. dried crushed red pepper*
½   *tsp. orange zest*

Sauté first 3 ingredients in hot oil in a large skillet 6 to 7 minutes or until tender. Add vinegar and next 3 ingredients to skillet, and sauté 2 minutes. Cool completely (30 minutes). Serve immediately, or refrigerate up to 1 week.

CARROT-GINGER PUREE

MAKES: 6 TO 8 SERVINGS ■ **HANDS-ON TIME:** 25 MIN.
TOTAL TIME: 55 MIN.

2   *lb. carrots, coarsely chopped (about 4 cups)*
2   *cups milk*
2   *Tbsp. sugar*
2   *tsp. grated fresh ginger or ½ tsp. ground ginger*
1   *tsp. table salt*
⅛   *tsp. ground cinnamon*
1   *Tbsp. butter*
1   *tsp. loosely packed orange zest*
Garnish: chopped fresh chives

1. Bring carrots and milk to a boil in a medium saucepan over medium heat. Reduce heat to low, and stir in sugar and next 3 ingredients. Simmer, stirring often, 25 minutes or until carrots are tender.
2. Transfer mixture to a blender, reserving ½ cup cooking liquid. Add butter and orange zest to carrot mixture, and process until smooth, stopping to scrape down sides as needed. Add reserved cooking liquid, if necessary, 1 Tbsp. at a time, and process to desired consistency. Serve immediately or chilled. Refrigerate in an airtight container up to 3 days.

Note: *Organic milk may curdle while simmering. Don't worry, it will smooth out when processed in the blender.*

HOT POTATO SALAD

MAKES: 6 TO 8 SERVINGS ■ **HANDS-ON TIME:** 20 MIN.
TOTAL TIME: 2 HOURS

1   *lb. processed cheese (such as Velveeta)*
8   *baking potatoes (about 4 lb.)*
1½   *cups mayonnaise*
1   *cup half-and-half*
½   *cup chopped yellow onion*
1   *cup sliced pimiento-stuffed Spanish olives*
6   *bacon slices, cut into 2-inch pieces*

1. Freeze cheese 45 minutes to 1 hour. Meanwhile, cook potatoes in boiling water to cover 25 to 30 minutes or

ASPARAGUS WITH
RED PEPPER CHOW-
CHOW

HOT POTATO
SALAD

CARROT-GINGER
PUREE

until tender; drain and cool completely.
2. Peel potatoes, and cut into 1-inch cubes. Grate frozen cheese, using large holes of a box grater.
3. Preheat oven to 325°. Whisk together mayonnaise and half-and-half in a large bowl. Stir in onion, olives, potatoes, and cheese until blended. Add salt and

pepper to taste. Spoon into a 13- x 9-inch baking dish coated with cooking spray. Top with bacon pieces.
4. Bake at 325° for 55 minutes. Increase oven temperature to broil, and broil 5 minutes or until bacon is crisp. Let stand 5 minutes.

EASTER-EGG SHORTBREAD COOKIES

Because a large batch of the dough is tricky to work with, we don't recommend doubling this recipe.

MAKES: 2 DOZEN ∎ **HANDS-ON TIME:** 1 HOUR
TOTAL TIME: 4 HOURS, 10 MIN., INCLUDING ICING

2 **cups butter, softened**
2 **Tbsp. vanilla extract**
1½ **cups powdered sugar**
4 **cups all-purpose flour**
2 **tsp. baking powder**
Parchment paper
Thin Royal Icing

1. Beat butter and vanilla at medium speed with an electric mixer until creamy. Whisk together powdered sugar, flour, and baking powder. Gradually add sugar mixture to butter mixture, beating at low speed until blended. Flatten dough into a disk, and wrap in plastic wrap. Chill 1 hour to 3 days.
2. Preheat oven to 350°. Place dough on a lightly floured surface; roll to ¼-inch thickness. Cut with desired cookie cutters. Place 8 cookies ½ inch apart on a parchment-lined baking sheet.
3. Bake at 350° for 12 to 13 minutes or until edges are lightly browned. Cool on baking sheets 5 minutes. Transfer to wire racks; cool completely (about 20 minutes).
4. Decorate cookies with Thin Royal Icing (see box on right to learn the wet-on-wet icing technique). Let dry 1 hour.

Thin Royal Icing

Beat 1 (32-oz.) package powdered sugar (about 7 ½ cups); 4 tsp. meringue powder; and 10 Tbsp. warm water at high speed with a heavy-duty electric stand mixer, using whisk attachment, 5 minutes or until glossy. Stir in up to 2 Tbsp. more warm water, 1 tsp. at a time, until mixture reaches desired consistency. Stir in food coloring, if desired. Use immediately, or store at room temperature in airtight containers up to 1 week. Makes about 5 cups.

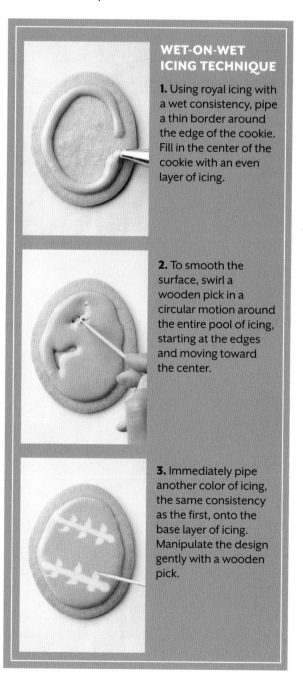

WET-ON-WET ICING TECHNIQUE

1. Using royal icing with a wet consistency, pipe a thin border around the edge of the cookie. Fill in the center of the cookie with an even layer of icing.

2. To smooth the surface, swirl a wooden pick in a circular motion around the entire pool of icing, starting at the edges and moving toward the center.

3. Immediately pipe another color of icing, the same consistency as the first, onto the base layer of icing. Manipulate the design gently with a wooden pick.

MENU

Derby Julep

Roasted Brown-Butter Pecans with Rosemary

Watercress Canapés

Assorted Vegetables with Whipped
Lemon Aïoli

Fluffy Cream Cheese Biscuits

Ginger Ale-Brown Sugar Smoked Ham

Derby Truffles

KENTUCKY DERBY PARTY

The fastest two minutes in sports leaves plenty of time for ham biscuits, bourbon truffles, and flavorful juleps. Encourage your guests to dress in Derby-inspired attire, such as a wide-brimmed hat decorated with flowers or bows and a colorful sundress.

WATERCRESS
CANAPÉS

DERBY JULEP

MAKES: 1 SERVING ■ **HANDS-ON TIME:** 5 MIN.
TOTAL TIME: 5 MIN. (NOT INCLUDING SYRUP)

3 to 5 fresh mint leaves
2 Tbsp. Mint Syrup
Crushed ice
¼ cup bourbon
1 fresh mint sprig

Place leaves and Mint Syrup in a chilled julep cup, and muddle against sides of cup to release flavors. Pack cup tightly with crushed ice; add bourbon and mint sprig.

Mint Syrup

Boil 1½ cups sugar and 1½ cups water, stirring often, 2 to 3 minutes or until sugar dissolves. Remove from heat; add 15 fresh mint sprigs, and cool completely. Cover and chill 24 hours. Strain syrup; discard solids.

ROASTED BROWN-BUTTER PECANS WITH ROSEMARY

MAKES: 4 CUPS ■ **HANDS-ON TIME:** 15 MIN.
TOTAL TIME: 1 HOUR

¼ cup butter
4 cups pecan halves
2 tsp. kosher salt
2 tsp. sugar
1 Tbsp. chopped fresh rosemary
Garnish: fresh rosemary leaves

1. Preheat oven to 350°. Cook butter in a medium saucepan over medium heat, stirring constantly, 3 to 5 minutes or just until butter begins to turn golden brown. Immediately remove pan from heat, and stir in pecans. Arrange pecans in a single layer on a baking sheet. Sprinkle with salt and sugar.

2. Bake pecans at 350° for 10 to 12 minutes or until toasted and fragrant, stirring halfway through. Sprinkle with rosemary. Bake 2 more minutes. Cool completely on baking sheet (about 30 minutes). Store in an air-tight container.

WATERCRESS CANAPÉS

You can make the cream cheese mixture up to 2 days ahead.

MAKES: 3 TO 6 DOZEN ■ **HANDS-ON TIME:** 40 MIN.
TOTAL TIME: 40 MIN.

1 (8-oz.) package cream cheese, softened
2 Tbsp. sour cream
2 Tbsp. mayonnaise
1 cup lightly packed watercress
¼ cup firmly packed fresh parsley leaves
¼ tsp. salt
¼ tsp. pepper
18 white sandwich bread slices
Assorted vegetable slices and herbs

1. Pulse first 3 ingredients in a food processor until smooth. Add watercress and next 3 ingredients; process until finely chopped.

2. Spread 1 Tbsp. cream cheese mixture onto each bread slice. Top with assorted vegetable slices and herbs in a single layer, pressing lightly. Trim crusts from bread. Cut each bread slice into 4 squares or 2 rectangles.

ROASTED BROWN-BUTTER PECANS WITH ROSEMARY

WHIPPED LEMON AÏOLI

Indulgent and lightly flavored, this dip is the perfect partner to colorful spring veggies such as green and purple endive; assorted radishes; and blanched, chilled asparagus and haricots verts (tiny green beans).

MAKES: ABOUT 2½ CUPS ▪ **HANDS-ON TIME:** 10 MIN.
TOTAL TIME: 10 MIN.

1   garlic clove
1   cup mayonnaise
2   tsp. lemon zest
1   Tbsp. lemon juice
¾   cup heavy cream
Assorted vegetables

1. Finely grate garlic into mayonnaise using a fine grater or zester. Stir in lemon zest and juice.
2. Beat cream at high speed with an electric mixer until medium peaks form. Add mayonnaise mixture, and beat until smooth. Season with salt to taste. Serve immediately with assorted vegetables, or cover and chill up to 1 day.

JULIAN'S OLD FASHIONED

Place 1 or 2 brown sugar cubes on a cocktail napkin. Sprinkle 2 or 3 drops orange bitters and 2 or 3 drops Angostura bitters over sugar cubes. (Napkin will soak up excess bitters.) Transfer cubes to a 10-oz. old-fashioned glass. Add 1 fresh orange slice and a few drops of bourbon to glass. Mash sugar cubes and orange slice, using a muddler, until sugar is almost dissolved. (Avoid mashing the rind; doing so will release a bitter flavor.) Add 1½ to 2 oz. bourbon, and fill glass with ice cubes. Stir until well chilled. Add more bourbon, if desired.

FLUFFY CREAM CHEESE BISCUITS

Three leavening ingredients—yeast, baking powder, and baking soda—ensure light biscuits every time. Serve with a variety of chutneys.

MAKES: ABOUT 18 BISCUITS ▪ **HANDS-ON TIME:** 15 MIN.
TOTAL TIME: 45 MIN.

1   (¼-oz.) envelope active dry yeast
¼   cup warm water (105° to 115°)
5   cups all-purpose flour
2   Tbsp. sugar
1   Tbsp. baking powder
1   tsp. baking soda
1   tsp. salt
1   (8-oz.) package cold cream cheese, cut into pieces
½   cup cold butter, cut into pieces
1¼ cups buttermilk
Parchment paper
2   Tbsp. butter, melted

1. Preheat oven to 400°. Combine yeast and warm water in a small bowl; let stand 5 minutes.
2. Meanwhile, whisk together flour and next 4 ingredients in a large bowl; cut cream cheese and cold butter into flour mixture with a pastry blender or fork until crumbly.
3. Combine yeast mixture and buttermilk, and add to flour mixture, stirring just until dry ingredients are moistened. Turn dough out onto a lightly floured surface, and knead lightly 6 to 8 times (about 30 seconds to 1 minute), sprinkling with up to ¼ cup additional flour as needed to prevent sticking.
4. Roll dough to ¾-inch thickness. Cut with a 2 ½-inch round cutter, rerolling scraps once. Arrange biscuits on 2 parchment paper-lined baking sheets.
5. Bake at 400° for 13 to 15 minutes or until golden brown. Brush with melted butter.

FLUFFY CREAM
CHEESE BISCUITS

GINGER ALE- BROWN
SUGAR SMOKED
HAM

WHIPPED
LEMON AÏOLI

GINGER ALE-BROWN SUGAR SMOKED HAM

Grab a bottle of your favorite spicy (or "hot") ginger ale (such as Blenheim from South Carolina, Buffalo Rock from Alabama, or a spicy Jamaican-style ginger beer) to use in this recipe.

MAKES: 16 TO 18 APPETIZER SERVINGS ■ **HANDS-ON TIME:** 15 MIN.
TOTAL TIME: 4 HOURS, 50 MIN.

1   (8- to 9-lb.) smoked, ready-to-cook bone-in ham
2   (12-oz.) bottles or cans spicy ginger ale
½   cup bourbon
¼   cup firmly packed dark brown sugar
2   tsp. coarsely ground black pepper
½   tsp. kosher salt
½   tsp. dry mustard
¼   tsp. ground red pepper

1. Preheat oven to 325°. Remove skin from ham, and trim fat to ¼-inch thickness. Make shallow cuts in fat 1 inch apart in a diamond pattern. Place ham, fat side up, in a roasting pan; add ginger ale and bourbon to pan. Cover loosely with foil.
2. Bake, covered, at 325° for 4 to 4 ½ hours or until a meat thermometer inserted into ham registers 140°, basting with pan juices every 30 minutes.
3. Stir together brown sugar and next 4 ingredients. Remove ham from oven; uncover and sprinkle sugar mixture over ham, lightly pressing mixture into fat.
4. Bake, uncovered, at 325° for 20 to 25 minutes or until crust is browned and a meat thermometer registers 145°. Transfer ham to a cutting board, and let stand 15 minutes before carving.

DERBY TRUFFLES

Serve these make-ahead gems with bakery macarons and/or sugar cookies on a tiered stand.

MAKES: ABOUT 3 DOZEN ■ **HANDS-ON TIME:** 35 MIN.
TOTAL TIME: 4 HOURS, 35 MIN.

3   (4-oz.) bittersweet chocolate baking bars, chopped
1½ Tbsp. cold butter, cubed
2   tsp. vanilla extract
9   Tbsp. heavy cream
¼   cup bourbon
1   (5.3-oz.) package pure butter shortbread cookies, crushed
2   cups finely chopped roasted, salted pecans
Wax paper

1. Combine first 3 ingredients in a large glass bowl. Cook cream and bourbon in a small saucepan over medium heat 3 to 4 minutes or until mixture is hot but not boiling. (Mixture will steam, and bubbles will form around edge of pan.) Pour cream mixture over chocolate. Let stand 1 minute.
2. Stir chocolate mixture until melted and smooth. (If mixture doesn't melt completely, microwave at HIGH 30 seconds. Stir in crushed cookies. Cover and chill 3 hours or until firm. (Mixture can be prepared and chilled up to 2 days ahead.)
3. Shape mixture into 1-inch balls (about 2 tsp. per ball). Roll in chopped pecans. Place on wax paper-lined baking sheets. Chill 1 hour. Store in an airtight container in refrigerator up to 5 days.

DERBY TRUFFLES

MENU

Iced Hibiscus Sweet Tea

Pink Cadillac Margaritas

Spiced Roasted Chili Peanuts and Pepitas

Chicken Enchiladas with Tomatillo Salsa

Chipotle Shrimp Cocktail

Mexican Chocolate Ice-Cream Pie

CINCO DE MAYO FIESTA

Spice up your Cinco de Mayo party with these crowd-pleasing dishes that can be made in advance, giving you more time to enjoy your guests. Accent your table setting with south-of-the-border-inspired decorations such as sombreros, maracas, and colorful tissue paper flowers.

ICED HIBISCUS SWEET TEA

MAKES: 7 CUPS ■ **HANDS-ON TIME:** 5 MIN.
TOTAL TIME: 2 HOURS, 20 MIN.

8   regular-size hibiscus tea bags
¾   cup sugar
1   navel orange, sliced
1   lime, sliced
3   cups ginger ale, chilled

Bring 4 cups water to a boil in a 2-qt. saucepan. Remove from heat, and add tea bags. Cover and steep 10 minutes. Discard tea bags. Stir in sugar until dissolved; add orange and lime slices. Cover and chill 2 to 6 hours. Stir in ginger ale, and serve over ice.

Note: *We tested with Celestial Seasonings Red Zinger Herbal Tea.*

PINK CADILLAC MARGARITAS

Mix up batches of margaritas 3 to 4 hours before the party starts, and chill in decorative pitchers, ready to shake and serve when guests arrive.

MAKES: 3¼ CUPS ■ **HANDS-ON TIME:** 10 MIN.
TOTAL TIME: 10 MIN.

1   cup tequila
1   cup fresh lime juice
½   cup powdered sugar
½   cup orange liqueur
½   cup cranberry juice

Stir together all ingredients until sugar is dissolved. Pour desired amount of mixture into a cocktail shaker filled with ice cubes. Cover with lid, and shake 30 seconds. Strain into chilled cocktail glasses. Repeat with remaining mixture. Serve immediately (or make ahead; see party prep shortcut above).

Note: *We tested with Cointreau orange liqueur.*

VIBRANT TERESITAS, OR MEXICAN TISSUE PAPER FLOWERS (AVAILABLE ON LATINWORKSCO.COM), SET A FESTIVE MOOD.

SPICED ROASTED CHILI PEANUTS AND PEPITAS

MAKES: ABOUT 3 CUPS ■ **HANDS-ON TIME:** 10 MIN.
TOTAL TIME: 40 MIN.

2   cups unsalted, dry-roasted peanuts
2   Tbsp. butter, melted
2   Tbsp. light brown sugar
2   tsp. chili powder
½   tsp. ground cinnamon
¼   tsp. ground red pepper
1   cup roasted, salted shelled pumpkin seeds (pepitas)

1. Preheat oven to 350°. Stir together dry-roasted peanuts and melted butter in a medium bowl.
2. Stir together brown sugar and next 3 ingredients. Add to peanut mixture, tossing to coat. Place peanuts in a single layer on a lightly greased baking sheet.
3. Bake at 350° for 10 to 15 minutes or until golden brown, stirring once. Remove from oven, and stir in pumpkin seeds. Cool completely in pan on a wire rack (about 20 minutes).

TAKE IT OUTSIDE
If you're planning on taking the party outdoors, a galvanized tub keeps drinks ice cold and adds a rustic touch.

CHICKEN ENCHILADAS

For added flavor, char one side of the tortillas directly over gas flames for a few seconds using tongs.

MAKES: 6 TO 8 SERVINGS   **HANDS-ON TIME:** 25 MIN.
TOTAL TIME: 2 HOURS, 45 MIN., INCLUDING SALSA

1   cup diced sweet onion
3   garlic cloves, minced
1   Tbsp. canola oil
2   cups chopped fresh baby spinach
2   (4.5-oz.) cans chopped green chiles, drained
3   cups shredded cooked chicken
1   (8-oz.) package ⅓-less-fat cream cheese, cubed
     and softened
2   cups (8 oz.) shredded pepper Jack cheese
⅓   cup chopped fresh cilantro
8   (8-inch) soft taco-size flour tortillas
Vegetable cooking spray
Tomatillo Salsa

1. Preheat oven to 350°. Sauté onion and garlic in hot oil in a large skillet over medium heat 5 minutes or until tender. Add spinach and green chiles; sauté 1 to 2 minutes or until spinach is wilted. Stir in chicken and next 3 ingredients, and cook, stirring constantly, 5 minutes or until cheeses melt. Add table salt and freshly ground black pepper to taste. Spoon about ¾ cup chicken mixture down center of each tortilla; roll up tortillas.
2. Place rolled tortillas, seam sides down, in a lightly greased 13- x 9-inch baking dish. Lightly coat tortillas with cooking spray.
3. Bake at 350° for 30 to 35 minutes or until golden brown. Top enchiladas with Tomatillo Salsa.

Make Ahead: Prepare recipe as directed through Step 2. Cover and chill overnight. Let stand at room temperature 30 minutes. Uncover and proceed as directed in Step 3.

Tomatillo Salsa

Stir together 2 cups diced tomatillo; ⅓ cup sliced green onions; ⅓ cup lightly packed fresh cilantro leaves; 1 jalapeño pepper, seeded and minced; 1 Tbsp. fresh lime juice; and ½ tsp. table salt. Cover and chill 1 to 4 hours. Let stand at room temperature 30 minutes. Stir in 1 cup diced avocado just before serving. Makes 3 cups.

CHIPOTLE SHRIMP COCKTAIL

MAKES: 8 SERVINGS ■ **HANDS-ON TIME:** 20 MIN.
TOTAL TIME: 12 HOURS, 20 MIN.

1 large red onion
1 medium-size red bell pepper
1 medium-size yellow bell pepper
2 lb. peeled and deveined, large cooked shrimp with tails
1 cup ketchup
½ cup chopped fresh cilantro
½ cup fresh lime juice
3 Tbsp. orange zest
½ cup fresh orange juice
2 to 3 canned chipotle peppers in adobo sauce, chopped

1. Cut onion and bell peppers into thin strips; layer with shrimp in a large zip-top plastic freezer bag.
2. Whisk together ketchup and next 5 ingredients; pour over shrimp mixture. Seal and chill 12 to 24 hours, turning bag occasionally. Serve with a slotted spoon.

MEXICAN CHOCOLATE ICE-CREAM PIE

MAKES: 8 SERVINGS **HANDS-ON TIME:** 30 MIN.
TOTAL TIME: 10 HOURS, 50 MIN.

3 cups cinnamon graham cracker crumbs (about 22 whole crackers), divided
½ cup butter, melted
¼ tsp. ground red pepper
1 (4-oz.) semisweet chocolate baking bar, finely chopped
1 (3.5-oz.) package roasted glazed pecan pieces
1 pt. chocolate ice cream, softened
1 pt. coffee ice cream, softened
1 cup whipping cream
¼ cup coffee liqueur

1. Preheat oven to 350°. Stir together 2½ cups cinnamon graham cracker crumbs and next 2 ingredients; firmly press mixture on bottom and up sides of a lightly greased 9-inch pie plate. Bake 10 to 12 minutes or until lightly browned. Cool completely on a wire rack (about 30 minutes).
2. Stir together semisweet chocolate, pecan pieces, and remaining ½ cup cinnamon graham cracker crumbs. Reserve ½ cup chocolate-pecan mixture to top pie.
3. Spread chocolate ice cream in bottom of prepared crust; top with remaining chocolate-pecan mixture. Freeze 30 minutes. Spread coffee ice cream over chocolate mixture. Cover and freeze 8 hours.
4. Beat whipping cream and coffee liqueur at medium speed with an electric mixer until stiff peaks form. Spread whipped cream mixture over pie; sprinkle with reserved ½ cup chocolate-pecan mixture. Cover and freeze 1 hour or until whipped cream is firm. Let stand 10 to 15 minutes before serving.

CHIPOTLE SHRIMP COCKTAIL

**MEXICAN CHOCOLATE
ICE-CREAM PIE**

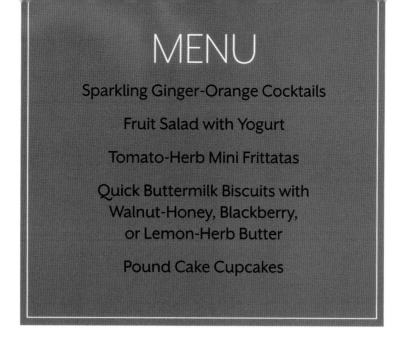

MENU

Sparkling Ginger-Orange Cocktails

Fruit Salad with Yogurt

Tomato-Herb Mini Frittatas

Quick Buttermilk Biscuits with
Walnut-Honey, Blackberry,
or Lemon-Herb Butter

Pound Cake Cupcakes

BRIDAL SHOWER

Celebrate a bride-to-be with this classic Southern luncheon menu. Create a gorgeous centerpiece with fresh roses in shades of pink set against a light blue tablecloth.

SPARKLING
GINGER-ORANGE
COCKTAILS

TOMATO-HERB
MINI FRITTATAS

QUICK BUTTERMILK
BISCUITS

SPARKLING GINGER-ORANGE COCKTAILS

MAKES: ABOUT 23 CUPS ■ **HANDS-ON TIME:** 10 MIN.
TOTAL TIME: 10 MIN.

1   Tbsp. finely grated ginger
2   (750-milliliter) bottles chilled sparkling wine
1   (89-oz.) container orange juice
1   (46-oz.) can chilled pineapple juice

1. Place ginger in a piece of cheesecloth, and squeeze juice from ginger into a large pitcher; discard cheesecloth and solids.
2. Stir sparkling wine, orange juice, and pineapple juice into ginger juice. Serve over ice.

FRUIT SALAD WITH YOGURT

MAKES: 8 SERVINGS ■ **HANDS-ON TIME:** 30 MIN.
TOTAL TIME: 30 MIN.

4   cups fresh pineapple chunks
1   qt. strawberries, hulled and sliced in half
3   cups seedless green grapes
2   mangoes, peeled and sliced
2   (4-oz.) containers fresh raspberries
2   cups Greek yogurt
1   Tbsp. dark brown sugar
1   Tbsp. honey

Toss together first 5 ingredients in a large serving bowl. Spoon yogurt into a separate serving bowl; sprinkle yogurt with sugar, and drizzle with honey. Serve fruit with yogurt mixture.

TOMATO-HERB MINI FRITTATAS

Transferring the bottom baking sheet to the middle rack during the last few minutes of cooking time allows the tops of the frittatas to brown slightly.

MAKES: 8 SERVINGS ■ **HANDS-ON TIME:** 15 MIN.
TOTAL TIME: 30 MIN.

12 large eggs
1   cup half-and-half
½   tsp. table salt
¼   tsp. freshly ground black pepper
2   Tbsp. chopped fresh chives
1   Tbsp. chopped fresh parsley
1   tsp. chopped fresh oregano
1   pt. grape tomatoes, halved
1½ cups (6 oz.) shredded Italian three-cheese blend

1. Preheat oven to 450°. Process first 4 ingredients in a blender until blended. Stir together chives and next 2 ingredients in a small bowl. Place 8 lightly greased 4-inch (6-oz.) ramekins on 2 baking sheets; layer tomatoes, 1 cup cheese, and chive mixture in ramekins. Pour egg mixture over top, and sprinkle with remaining ½ cup cheese.
2. Bake at 450° for 7 minutes, placing 1 baking sheet on middle oven rack and other on lower oven rack. Switch baking sheets, and bake 7 to 8 more minutes or until set. Remove top baking sheet from oven; transfer bottom sheet to middle rack, and bake 1 to 2 more minutes or until lightly browned.

FRUIT SALAD WITH YOGURT

TOMATO-HERB MINI
FRITTATAS

QUICK BUTTERMILK BISCUITS

Fill biscuits with thinly sliced ham or spread with desired flavored butter.

MAKES: ABOUT 3 DOZEN ■ **HANDS-ON TIME:** 10 MIN.
TOTAL TIME: 22 MIN.

1   **cup shortening**
4   **cups self-rising soft-wheat flour**
1¾ **cups buttermilk**

1. Preheat oven to 425°. Cut shortening into flour with a pastry blender until crumbly. Add buttermilk, stirring just until dry ingredients are moistened.
2. Turn dough out onto a lightly floured surface, and knead lightly 4 or 5 times. Pat or roll dough to ¾-inch thickness, cut with a 1½-inch round cutter, and place on 2 lightly greased baking sheets.
3. Bake at 425° for 12 to 14 minutes or until lightly browned.

Freezing instructions: Place unbaked biscuits on pans in freezer for 30 minutes or until frozen. Transfer frozen biscuits to zip-top plastic freezer bags, and freeze up to 3 months. Bake frozen biscuits at 425° on lightly greased baking sheets 14 to 16 minutes or until lightly browned.

WALNUT-HONEY BUTTER

MAKES: ABOUT ¾ CUP ■ **HANDS-ON TIME:** 5 MIN.
TOTAL TIME: 25 MIN.

Bake ¼ cup finely chopped walnuts at 350° in a single layer in a pan 5 to 7 minutes or until lightly toasted, stirring halfway through. Cool 15 minutes. Stir together ½ cup softened butter, 2 Tbsp. honey, and walnuts.

BLACKBERRY BUTTER

MAKES: ABOUT ¾ CUP ■ **HANDS-ON TIME:** 5 MIN.
TOTAL TIME: 5 MIN.

Stir together ½ cup softened butter and 3 Tbsp. blackberry preserves.

LEMON-HERB BUTTER

MAKES: ABOUT ½ CUP ■ **HANDS-ON TIME:** 5 MIN.
TOTAL TIME: 5 MIN.

Stir together ½ cup softened butter, 2 tsp. lemon zest, 1 tsp. chopped fresh chives, 1 tsp. chopped fresh oregano, and 1 tsp. chopped fresh parsley.

WALNUT-HONEY BUTTER

BLACKBERRY BUTTER

LEMON-HERB BUTTER

POUND CAKE CUPCAKES

MAKES: 30 CUPCAKES ■ **HANDS-ON TIME:** 30 MIN.
TOTAL TIME: 1 HOUR, 55 MIN., NOT INCLUDING BLOSSOMS

1   *cup butter, softened*
2½ *cups sugar*
6   *large eggs*
3   *cups all-purpose flour*
1   *tsp. baking powder*
1   *(8-oz.) container mascarpone cheese, softened*
3   *tsp. vanilla extract, divided*
30 *paper baking cups*
9   *(2-oz.) vanilla candy coating squares, coarsely
     chopped*
½   *cup whipping cream*
2   *Tbsp. butter, softened*
Sky blue food coloring paste
Hydrangea Blossoms

1. Preheat oven to 350°. Beat 1 cup butter at medium speed with an electric mixer until fluffy; gradually add sugar, beating well. Add eggs, 1 at a time, beating just until blended after each addition.

2. Stir together flour and baking powder. Add flour mixture to butter mixture alternately with mascarpone cheese, beginning and ending with flour mixture. Beat at low speed just until blended after each addition. Stir in 2 tsp. vanilla. Place 30 paper baking cups in 3 (12-cup) standard-size muffin pans; spoon batter into cups using a 4-Tbsp. (¼-cup) cookie scoop.

3. Bake at 350° for 20 to 23 minutes or until a wooden pick inserted in centers comes out clean. Remove from pans to wire racks, and cool completely.

4. Microwave vanilla candy coating and whipping cream in a 1-qt. microwave-safe bowl at MEDIUM (50% power) 1½ minutes. Stir mixture, and microwave 1 more minute or until candy coating is almost melted, gently stirring at 30-second intervals. Whisk until melted and smooth. (Do not overheat or overwhisk.) Whisk in 2 Tbsp. softened butter and remaining 1 tsp. vanilla. Tint with desired amount of food coloring paste.

5. Working quickly, dip tops of cupcakes in candy mixture. Place right-side-up on a wire rack. (If mixture begins to harden, microwave 10 to 15 seconds, and stir until smooth.) Top with blossoms.

Hydrangea Blossoms

Ready-to-use fondant is just as easy to cut and shape as Play-Doh. A hydrangea gumpaste cutter set (petalcrafts.com) adds realistic details. Find fondant and color dust at crafts stores or wilton.com.

1. Dust work surface with cornstarch. Thinly roll fondant; stamp with petal veiner included in kit.

2. Cut blossoms with petal cutter. Press petal edges between fingertips; shape and let harden on candy gummy rings until firm enough to lift.

3. Accent petals with dark blue color dust. Mold anthers; let harden, and brush with yellow dust. Dot petal centers with corn syrup; add anthers.

MENU

Sparkling Pink Lemonade Punch

Deviled Eggs with Smoked Salmon and
Cream Cheese

Scalloped Potato and
Herb Tart

Strawberries-and-Cream
Sheet Cake

BABY SHOWER

*Shower a new mom-to-be with gifts and well-wishes. Decorate with vivid shades
of blue or pink if you're in the know, or keep things neutral with yellow, green, or all white
to play it safe. This menu of tasty little morsels is perfectly fitting for the occasion.*

SPARKLING PINK LEMONADE PUNCH

SPARKLING PINK LEMONADE PUNCH

Tangy pink lemonade and tart cranberry juice come together for a refreshingly bubbly drink. Fresh mint sprigs add a touch of color.

MAKES: ABOUT 9 CUPS   **HANDS-ON TIME:** 5 MIN.
TOTAL TIME: 1 HOUR, 5 MIN.

1   (12-oz.) can frozen pink lemonade concentrate, thawed
4   cups white cranberry juice cocktail
1   qt. club soda, chilled
Garnish: fresh mint sprigs

1. Stir together lemonade concentrate and cranberry juice cocktail in a large pitcher. Cover and chill at least 1 hour or up to 24 hours. Stir in club soda just before serving.

DEVILED EGGS WITH SMOKED SALMON AND CREAM CHEESE

MAKES: 12 SERVINGS   **HANDS-ON TIME:** 18 MIN.
TOTAL TIME: 40 MIN.

6   large eggs
3   Tbsp. minced smoked salmon (about 1 oz.)
3   Tbsp. minced green onions
3   Tbsp. softened cream cheese
1   Tbsp. sour cream
1   tsp. Dijon mustard
2   tsp. lemon juice
¼   tsp. salt
⅛   tsp. ground red pepper
Garnishes: fresh dill, smoked salmon slivers, sweet paprika

1. Place eggs and enough water to cover in a saucepan over medium heat; bring to a boil. Cover, remove from heat, and let stand 15 minutes. Drain; return eggs to saucepan, and add enough cold water and ice to cover. Let cool. Remove shells from eggs, halve each egg lengthwise, and scrape yolks into a bowl. Reserve egg whites.
2. Combine yolks, salmon, and next 7 ingredients, mashing with a fork until well blended. Spoon filling into reserved whites, cover loosely with plastic wrap, and refrigerate up to 2 days.

SCALLOPED POTATO AND HERB TART

MAKES: 6 TO 8 SERVINGS **HANDS-ON TIME:** 30 MIN.
TOTAL TIME: 2 HOURS, INCLUDING PASTRY

Buttery Flaky Pastry

- 1 medium-size russet potato (about 12 oz.), peeled and cut into ⅟₁₆-inch-thick slices
- 1½ tsp. table salt, divided
- 6 green onions, cut into 1-inch pieces (about 1 cup)
- ½ cup coarsely chopped fresh flat-leaf parsley
- ¼ cup coarsely chopped fresh chives
- ½ to 1 Tbsp. coarsely chopped fresh dill
- 1 cup half-and-half
- 2 large eggs
- 1 large egg yolk
- 1 tsp. fresh thyme leaves
- ½ tsp. freshly ground pepper
- 1 cup (4 oz.) shredded Gruyère cheese
- ¼ cup (1 oz.) freshly shredded Parmesan cheese

1. Prepare Buttery Flaky Pastry.
2. Preheat oven 350°. Bring potatoes, 1 tsp. salt, and water to cover to a boil in a large skillet over medium-high heat; cook 5 to 7 minutes or until tender. Drain potatoes, and pat dry with paper towels. Cool 10 minutes.
3. Cook onions in boiling salted water to cover in a small saucepan 2 to 3 minutes or until tender. Drain well, and press between paper towels.
4. Stir together parsley and next 2 ingredients in a small bowl.
5. Whisk together half-and-half, next 4 ingredients, half of parsley mixture, and remaining ½ tsp. salt.
6. Spread half of potatoes in bottom of pastry crust. Top with half of Gruyère cheese, half of cooked onions, and half of egg mixture; repeat layers once. Sprinkle with Parmesan cheese.
7. Bake at 350° on an aluminum foil-lined baking sheet 40 to 45 minutes or until center is set. Let stand 10 minutes. Sprinkle with remaining parsley mixture. Serve warm or at room temperature.

Buttery Flaky Pastry

MAKES: 1 9-INCH PASTRY SHELL **HANDS-ON TIME:** 15 MIN.
TOTAL TIME: 2 HOURS, 20 MIN.

- 2½ cups all-purpose flour
- ½ tsp. table salt
- ½ cup cold butter, cut into small cubes
- ¼ to ½ cup ice-cold water
- Parchment paper

1. Pulse flour and salt in a food processor 3 or 4 times or until combined. Add butter; pulse 5 or 6 times or until mixture resembles coarse meal. With processor running, gradually add ¼ cup ice-cold water, and process just until dough forms a ball and pulls away from sides of bowl, adding up to ¼ cup more ice-cold water if needed.
2. Gently form dough into a flat disk; wrap in plastic wrap, and chill 1 hour to 2 days.
3. Preheat oven to 400°. Roll dough into a 12-inch circle (about ⅛ inch thick) on a lightly floured surface. Fit into a lightly greased 9-inch round tart pan with removable bottom, pressing dough on bottom and up sides into fluted edges.
4. Line dough with parchment paper, and fill with pie weights or dried beans.
5. Bake at 400° for 20 minutes. Remove weights and parchment paper, and bake 15 to 20 more minutes or until bottom is golden. Transfer to a wire rack. Cool completely (about 30 minutes).

COLOR POP

Welcome guests with a whimsical, eye-catching centerpiece that sets a cheery mood. Here, retro meets traditional—a pink flamingo pops up from a colorful arrangement of fresh spring flowers.

STRAWBERRIES-AND-CREAM SHEET CAKE

MAKES: 10 TO 12 SERVINGS **HANDS-ON TIME:** 35 MIN.
TOTAL TIME: 2 HOURS, 50 MIN.

1   cup butter, softened
2   cups sugar
2   large eggs
2   tsp. fresh lemon juice
1   tsp. vanilla extract
2½ cups cake flour
2   Tbsp. strawberry-flavored gelatin
½   tsp. baking soda
¼   tsp. table salt
1   cup buttermilk
⅔   cup chopped fresh strawberries
Shortening
Parchment paper
Strawberry Frosting
Garnish: fresh strawberries

1. Preheat oven to 350°. Beat butter at medium speed with an electric mixer until creamy; gradually add sugar, beating 4 to 5 minutes or until light and fluffy. Add eggs, 1 at a time, beating until blended after each addition. Beat in lemon juice and vanilla.

2. Stir together flour and next 3 ingredients; add flour mixture to butter mixture alternately with buttermilk, beginning and ending with flour mixture. Beat at low speed just until blended. Stir in strawberries.

3. Grease (with shortening) and flour a 13- x 9-inch pan; line with parchment paper, allowing 2 to 3 inches to extend over long sides. Lightly grease paper with cooking spray. Spread batter in prepared pan.

4. Bake at 350° for 30 to 40 minutes or until a wooden pick inserted in center comes out clean. Cool in pan on a wire rack 30 minutes. Lift cake from pan, using parchment paper sides as handles. Invert cake onto wire rack; gently remove parchment paper. Cool completely (about 1 hour). Spread Strawberry Frosting on top and sides of cake.

Strawberry Frosting

MAKES: ABOUT 5 CUPS **HANDS-ON TIME:** 15 MIN.
TOTAL TIME: 15 MIN.

1   (8-oz.) package cream cheese, softened
⅔   cup sugar, divided
⅔   cup chopped fresh strawberries
1   drop of pink food coloring gel (optional)
1½ cups heavy cream
3   Tbsp. fresh lemon juice

1. Beat cream cheese and ⅓ cup sugar with an electric mixer until smooth; add strawberries and food coloring, if desired; beat until blended.

2. Beat cream and lemon juice at medium speed until foamy; increase speed to medium-high, and slowly add remaining ⅓ cup sugar, beating until stiff peaks form. Fold half of cream mixture into cheese mixture; fold in remaining cream mixture. Use immediately.

**TOMATO-BASIL
BISQUE**

MENU

hot tea and coffee

Tomato-Basil Bisque

Tea Sandwiches

Green Pea Hummus with
crudités and crostini

Banana Pudding
Cheesecake

GRADUATION LUNCHEON

*Say farewell to typical college chow with a sophisticated post-graduation luncheon.
Classy tea sandwiches and a nostalgic banana pudding-inspired cheesecake make
for a celebration your graduates will remember.*

TOMATO-BASIL BISQUE

MAKES: ABOUT 7 CUPS ■ **HANDS-ON TIME:** 15 MIN.
TOTAL TIME: 15 MIN.

2   *(10 ¾-oz.) cans tomato soup*
1   *(14 ½-oz.) can diced fire-roasted tomatoes*
2½ *cups buttermilk*
2   *Tbsp. chopped fresh basil*
¼   *tsp. freshly ground pepper*
*Toppings: fresh basil leaves, freshly ground pepper,
    Parmesan cheese*

Cook first 5 ingredients in a 3-qt. saucepan over medium heat, stirring often, 6 to 8 minutes or until thoroughly heated. Serve immediately with desired toppings.

CELEBRATE WITH FLOWERS
White ranunculus, roses, clematis, geranium foliage, and maidenhair ferns double as a bouquet for grads or as a party table centerpiece.

CURRIED SHRIMP

ORANGE AND
CRANBERRY

GOAT CHEESE
AND PECAN

CUCUMBER AND
STRAWBERRY

HAM SALAD

EGG SALAD

TEA SANDWICHES

Prepare your favorite fillings up to a day ahead. Plan on ¼ cup filling for each whole sandwich. Freeze bread slices. Trim crusts with a long serrated knife after sandwiches are filled; cut each sandwich into 4 triangles. Make sandwiches up to 4 hours ahead. Place in an airtight container, cover with wax paper and a damp paper towel, and refrigerate.

Ham Salad

MAKES: ABOUT 3 CUPS ■ **HANDS-ON TIME:** 15 MIN.
TOTAL TIME: 15 MIN.

Process 1 lb. chopped baked ham, in batches, in a food processor until coarsely ground, stopping to scrape down sides as needed. Place ground ham in a bowl, and stir in 3 hard-cooked eggs, peeled and grated; ⅔ cup mayonnaise; and ½ cup finely chopped sweet-hot pickled okra. Add salt and pepper to taste. Spread on rye bread slices.

Curried Shrimp

MAKES: ABOUT 3 CUPS ■ **HANDS-ON TIME:** 15 MIN.
TOTAL TIME: 15 MIN.

Stir together 2½ cups finely chopped peeled and deveined, cooked shrimp (about 1 lb. of any size); ½ cup finely diced celery; ½ cup toasted sweetened flaked coconut; 1½ (8-oz.) packages cream cheese, softened; 3 Tbsp. minced green onions; 1 Tbsp. freshly grated ginger; 1½ tsp. curry powder; ¼ tsp. salt; and ¼ tsp. ground red pepper until well blended. Spread on white bread.
Curried Chicken: Substitute 2½ cups finely chopped cooked chicken for shrimp. Prepare recipe as directed. Spread on raisin bread.

Cucumber and Strawberry

MAKES: ABOUT 2 CUPS ■ **HANDS-ON TIME:** 15 MIN.
TOTAL TIME: 15 MIN.

Stir together 1 (8-oz.) package cream cheese, softened; ½ cup peeled, seeded, and finely chopped cucumber; ⅓ cup mayonnaise; ¼ cup minced red onion; 3 Tbsp. finely chopped fresh basil; ½ tsp. freshly ground pepper; and ¼ tsp. salt. Spread on white bread; sandwich with diced fresh strawberries.

Goat Cheese and Pecan

MAKES: ABOUT 2 CUPS ■ **HANDS-ON TIME:** 15 MIN.
TOTAL TIME: 15 MIN.

Stir together 4 oz. each softened cream cheese and goat cheese, 1 cup (4 oz.) shredded white Cheddar cheese, ½ cup finely chopped toasted pecans, and 2 Tbsp. chopped fresh cilantro. Spread on whole wheat bread slices. Spread a thin layer of red pepper jelly on an equal number of whole wheat bread slices; sandwich cream cheese mixture slices with pepper jelly slices.

Orange and Cranberry

MAKES: ABOUT 2 CUPS ■ **HANDS-ON TIME:** 15 MIN.
TOTAL TIME: 15 MIN.

Stir together 1 (8-oz.) package cream cheese, softened; ⅔ cup sweetened dried cranberries; ⅓ cup orange marmalade; and ½ cup chopped toasted pecans. Spread on pumpernickel bread; sandwich with thinly sliced smoked turkey and fresh arugula.

Egg Salad

MAKES: ABOUT 3 CUPS ■ **HANDS-ON TIME:** 15 MIN.
TOTAL TIME: 15 MIN.

Stir together 8 hard-cooked eggs, peeled and grated; ⅔ cup mayonnaise; ½ cup finely diced celery; ¼ cup finely chopped chives; 2 Tbsp. minced red onion; 1 Tbsp. chopped fresh tarragon; 1 tsp. freshly ground pepper; and ½ tsp. seasoned salt. Spread on whole grain bread slices. Spread mayonnaise on an equal number of whole grain bread slices. Sandwich egg salad slices and mayonnaise slices with fresh watercress.

GREEN PEA
HUMMUS

GREEN PEA HUMMUS

MAKES: ABOUT ¾ CUP ■ **HANDS-ON TIME:** 5 MIN.
TOTAL TIME: 8 MIN.

1   cup fresh or frozen, thawed sweet peas
¼   cup olive oil
2   Tbsp. chopped fresh mint
1   garlic clove
¼   tsp. salt
*Crudités (such as baby bell peppers, radish halves,
    sugar snap peas, and endive leaves) and crostini*

Cook peas in boiling salted water to cover 1 to 3 minutes or just until crisp-tender; drain. Plunge sweet peas into ice water to stop the cooking process; drain. Pulse blanched sweet peas, olive oil, chopped fresh mint, garlic clove, and salt in a food processor 4 or 5 times or until smooth. Store in an airtight container in refrigerator up to 3 days. Serve with crudités (assorted vegetables) and crostini (toasted bread slices).

BANANA PUDDING CHEESECAKE

MAKES: 10 TO 12 SERVINGS ■ **HANDS-ON TIME:** 45 MIN.
TOTAL TIME: 11 HOURS, 10 MIN.

1½ cups finely crushed vanilla wafers
½   cup chopped pecans
¼   cup butter, melted
17 vanilla wafers
2   large ripe bananas, diced
1   Tbsp. lemon juice
2   Tbsp. light brown sugar
3   (8-oz.) packages cream cheese, softened
1   cup granulated sugar
3   large eggs
2   tsp. vanilla extract
½   cup coarsely crushed vanilla wafers
*Garnishes: sweetened whipped cream, vanilla
    wafers, sliced bananas tossed in lemon juice*

1. Preheat oven to 350°. Stir together first 3 ingredients in a small bowl until well blended. Press mixture onto bottom of a greased and floured 9-inch springform pan. Stand 17 vanilla wafers around edge of pan (rounded sides against pan), pressing gently into crust to secure. Bake 10 minutes. Cool completely on a wire rack (about 30 minutes).
2. Combine bananas and lemon juice in a small saucepan. Stir in brown sugar. Cook over medium-high heat, stirring constantly, 1 minute or just until sugar has dissolved.
3. Beat cream cheese at medium speed with an electric mixer 3 minutes or until smooth. Gradually add granulated sugar, beating until blended. Add eggs, 1 at a time, beating just until yellow disappears after each addition. Beat in vanilla. Gently stir banana mixture into cream cheese mixture. Pour batter into prepared crust.
4. Bake at 350° for 45 to 55 minutes or until center is almost set. Remove cheesecake from oven; gently run a knife around edge of cheesecake to loosen. Sprinkle top of cheesecake with coarsely crushed wafers. Cool completely on a wire rack (about 1 hour). Cover and chill 8 hours.

BANANA PUDDING
CHEESECAKE

MENU

sweet tea

Fried Chicken Bites

Lemony Potato Salad

Spring Salad

Fresh Fruit

Strawberry Rhubarb
Handpies

MEMORIAL DAY PICNIC

Spread a big blanket on the lawn, and celebrate Memorial Day this year with a portable, easy-to-pack menu. A vintage wicker picnic basket paired with modern serving pieces gives an eclectic touch to a laid-back meal.

FRIED CHICKEN BITES

FRIED CHICKEN BITES

MAKES: 4 TO 6 SERVINGS ■ **HANDS-ON TIME:** 50 MIN.
TOTAL TIME: 50 MIN., PLUS 1 DAY FOR MARINATING

- 1½ *tsp. to 1 Tbsp. ground red pepper*
- 1½ *tsp. ground chipotle chile pepper*
- 1½ *tsp. garlic powder*
- 1½ *tsp. dried crushed red pepper*
- 1½ *tsp. ground black pepper*
- ¾ *tsp. salt*
- ½ *tsp. paprika*
- 2 *lb. skinned and boned chicken breasts*
- 2 *cups buttermilk*
- 3 *bread slices, toasted*
- 1 *cup all-purpose flour*
- *Peanut oil*
- *Blue cheese dressing or honey mustard dressing*

1. Combine first 7 ingredients in a small bowl; reserve half of spice mixture. Cut chicken into 1-inch pieces. Place chicken in a medium bowl, and toss with remaining spice mixture until coated. Stir in buttermilk; cover and chill 24 hours.
2. Tear bread into pieces, and place in a food processor with reserved spice mixture. Process until mixture resembles cornmeal. Stir in flour. Remove chicken pieces from buttermilk, discarding buttermilk. Dredge chicken in breadcrumb mixture.
3. Pour oil to depth of 2 inches in a Dutch oven; heat to 350°. Fry chicken, in batches, 6 to 7 minutes on each side or until golden brown and done. Drain on a wire rack over paper towels. Sprinkle with salt to taste. Serve warm or cold with blue cheese dressing or honey mustard.

LEMONY POTATO SALAD

MAKES: 6 SERVINGS ■ **HANDS-ON TIME:** 5 MIN.
TOTAL: 25 MIN.

- 2 *lb. red potatoes, cut into eighths*
- ¼ *cup olive oil*
- 3 *Tbsp. lemon juice*
- ¾ *tsp. salt*
- ½ *tsp. dry mustard*
- ¼ *tsp. freshly ground pepper*
- 3 *green onions, thinly sliced*
- 2 *Tbsp. chopped fresh parsley*

1. Bring potatoes and salted cold water to cover to a boil in a large Dutch oven; boil 15 to 17 minutes or just until tender. Drain and let cool 5 minutes.
2. Whisk together olive oil and next 4 ingredients in a large bowl. Add warm potatoes, green onions, and parsley; toss to coat. Serve at room temperature or chilled.

STRAWBERRY-RHUBARB
HAND PIES

SPRING SALSA

This colorful salsa works well over salad greens or in warm tortillas with grilled chicken.

MAKES: 3½ CUPS **HANDS-ON TIME:** 15 MIN.
TOTAL TIME: 15 MIN.

1½ cups cherry tomatoes, seeded and chopped
1 cup frozen whole kernel corn, thawed
¼ cup chopped red onion
2 Tbsp. chopped fresh cilantro
1 garlic clove, minced
1 jalapeño pepper, seeded and minced
2 Tbsp. fresh lime juice
Tortilla chips

Stir together first 7 ingredients. Season with salt and pepper to taste. Cover and chill until ready to serve (up to 3 hours). Serve with tortilla chips.

STRAWBERRY-RHUBARB HAND PIES

MAKES: 2 DOZEN **HANDS-ON TIME:** 1 HOUR, 25 MIN.
TOTAL TIME: 2 HOURS, 10 MIN.

¾ cup finely diced fresh strawberries
¾ cup finely diced rhubarb
1 Tbsp. cornstarch
6 Tbsp. sugar, divided
3 tsp. orange zest, divided
2¼ cups all-purpose flour
¼ tsp. salt
½ cup butter, cold
¼ cup shortening, chilled
3 Tbsp. ice-cold water
3 Tbsp. orange juice
Parchment paper
1 large egg yolk, beaten
1 Tbsp. whipping cream
Sugar

1. Combine strawberries, rhubarb, cornstarch, 2 Tbsp. sugar, and 1½ tsp. orange zest in a small bowl.
2. Preheat oven to 375°. Combine flour, salt, and remaining ¼ cup sugar in a large bowl. Cut in butter and shortening with a pastry blender until mixture resembles small peas. Stir in remaining 1½ tsp. orange zest. Drizzle with ice-cold water and orange juice. Stir with a fork until combined. (Mixture will be crumbly and dry.) Knead mixture lightly, and shape dough into a disk. Divide dough in half.
3. Roll half of dough to ⅛-inch thickness on a heavily floured surface. (Cover remaining dough with plastic wrap.) Cut with a 2¼-inch round cutter, rerolling scraps as needed. Place half of dough rounds 2 inches apart on parchment paper-lined baking sheets. Top with 1 rounded teaspoonful strawberry mixture. Dampen edges of dough with water, and top with remaining dough rounds, pressing edges to seal. Crimp edges with a fork, and cut a slit in top of each round for steam to escape. Repeat procedure with remaining dough and strawberry mixture.
4. Stir together egg yolk and cream; brush pies with egg wash. Sprinkle with sugar. Freeze pies 10 minutes.
5. Bake at 375° for 20 to 25 minutes or until lightly browned. Cool 10 minutes. Serve warm or at room temperature. Store in an airtight container up to 2 days.

FILL INEXPENSIVE, REUSABLE GLASS JARS WITH SPRING SALSA AND CHIPS FOR EASY CARRYING.

MENU

sweet tea

Beer-Battered Fried Fish

Grilled Corn-and-Butter
Bean Salad

Peach-Ginger Slaw

Hush Puppies

Peanut-Cola Cake

FATHER'S DAY
FISH FRY

*Dad is sure to love this seaside-inspired menu of fried fish and all the fixin's.
Create a beach theme in your backyard with nautical decorations such as
seashells, beach chairs, and tiki torches.*

BUTTERMILK-RANCH-HERB SAUCE

MALT VINEGAR MIGNONETTE

BEER-BATTERED FRIED FISH

BEER-BATTERED FRIED FISH

Serve with Buttermilk-Ranch-Herb Sauce or Malt Vinegar Mignonette.

MAKES: 8 SERVINGS **HANDS-ON TIME:** 30 MIN.
TOTAL TIME: 30 MIN.

Vegetable oil
2   *lb. grouper fillets, cut into pieces*
2   *tsp. table salt, divided*
½   *tsp. freshly ground black pepper*
1½   *cups all-purpose flour*
1½   *tsp. sugar*
1   *(12-oz.) bottle beer*
1   *tsp. hot sauce*

1. Pour oil to depth of 3 inches in a large Dutch oven; heat to 360°.
2. Meanwhile, sprinkle fish with 1 tsp. salt and pepper.
3. Whisk together flour, sugar, and remaining salt in a large bowl. Whisk in beer and hot sauce. Dip fish in batter, allowing excess batter to drip off.
4. Gently lower fish into hot oil using tongs (to prevent fish from sticking to Dutch oven). Fry fish, in 4 batches, 2 to 3 minutes on each side or until golden brown. Place fried fish on a wire rack in a jelly-roll pan; keep warm in a 200° oven until ready to serve.

Buttermilk-Ranch-Herb Sauce

MAKES: 1⅓ CUPS **HANDS-ON TIME:** 5 MIN.
TOTAL TIME: 5 MIN.

Whisk together 1 cup mayonnaise, ⅓ cup buttermilk, 1½ Tbsp. chopped fresh chives, 2 tsp. Ranch dressing mix, 1 tsp. lemon zest, 3 Tbsp. fresh lemon juice, ½ tsp. freshly ground black pepper, and ¼ tsp. table salt. Serve immediately, or cover and chill up to 2 days.

Malt Vinegar Mignonette

MAKES: 2 CUPS **HANDS-ON TIME:** 5 MIN.
TOTAL TIME: 5 MIN.

Stir together 2 cups malt vinegar, 1 large diced shallot, and ½ tsp. freshly ground black pepper in a small bowl. Serve immediately, or cover and chill up to 24 hours.

GRILLED CORN-AND-BUTTER BEAN SALAD

MAKES: 8 TO 10 SERVINGS   **HANDS-ON TIME:** 35 MIN.
TOTAL TIME: 3 HOURS, 20 MIN.

1   (16-oz.) package frozen butter beans
4   ears fresh corn, husks removed
1   large red onion, cut into thick slices
1   large red bell pepper, cut into thick rings
¾   cup mayonnaise
3   Tbsp. chopped fresh basil
1   garlic clove, pressed
1   tsp. table salt
1   tsp. Worcestershire sauce
½   tsp. freshly ground black pepper
1   cup halved grape tomatoes

1. Cook butter beans according to package directions; drain and cool completely (about 20 minutes).
2. Meanwhile, preheat grill to 350° to 400° (medium-high) heat. Grill corn, covered with grill lid, 15 minutes or until done, turning every 4 to 5 minutes. (Some kernels will begin to char and pop.) At the same time, grill onion and bell pepper, covered with grill lid, 5 minutes on each side or until tender. Cool all vegetables completely (about 20 minutes).
3. Cut corn kernels from cobs. Discard cobs. Chop onion and bell pepper into ½-inch pieces.
4. Stir together mayonnaise and next 5 ingredients. Stir in tomatoes, corn kernels, and onion and pepper pieces. Add salt to taste. Cover and chill 2 to 8 hours before serving. Store in refrigerator up to 3 days.

*Fresh butter beans may be substituted.

PEACH-GINGER SLAW

MAKES: 8 SERVINGS   **HANDS-ON TIME:** 20 MIN.
TOTAL TIME: 20 MIN.

3   Tbsp. pepper jelly
¼   cup rice wine vinegar
1   Tbsp. sesame oil
1   tsp. grated fresh ginger
⅓   cup canola oil
1   (16-oz.) package shredded coleslaw mix
2   large fresh peaches, unpeeled and coarsely chopped (about 2 cups)
1   cup chopped toasted pecans

1. Microwave jelly in a large microwave-safe bowl at HIGH 15 seconds. Whisk in vinegar and next 2 ingredients until blended. Gradually add canola oil in a slow, steady stream, whisking constantly until well blended.
2. Add coleslaw mix, and toss to coat. Gently stir in peaches. Stir in pecans; add table salt to taste. Serve immediately, or cover and chill up to 8 hours, stirring in pecans and table salt to taste just before serving.

GRILLED CORN-AND-BUTTER BEAN SALAD

PEACH-GINGER SLAW

HUSH PUPPIES

HUSH PUPPIES

MAKES: 8 TO 10 SERVINGS (ABOUT 2 DOZEN HUSH PUPPIES)
HANDS-ON TIME: 25 MIN. **TOTAL TIME:** 35 MIN.

Vegetable oil
1½ *cups self-rising white cornmeal mix*
¾ *cup self-rising flour*
¾ *cup diced sweet onion (about ½ medium onion)*
1½ *Tbsp. sugar*
1 *large egg, lightly beaten*
1¼ *cups buttermilk*

1. Pour oil to depth of 3 inches in a Dutch oven; heat to 375°. Combine cornmeal and next 3 ingredients. Add egg and buttermilk; stir just until moistened. Let stand 10 minutes.
2. Drop batter by rounded tablespoonfuls into hot oil, and fry, in 3 batches, 2 to 3 minutes on each side or until golden. Keep warm in a 200° oven.

PEANUT-COLA CAKE

MAKES: 12 SERVINGS **HANDS-ON TIME:** 20 MIN.
TOTAL TIME: 1 HOUR, INCLUDING FROSTING

1 *cup cola soft drink*
½ *cup buttermilk*
1 *cup butter, softened*
1¾ *cups sugar*
2 *large eggs, lightly beaten*
2 *tsp. vanilla extract*
2 *cups all-purpose flour*
¼ *cup unsweetened cocoa*
1 *tsp. baking soda*
Peanut Butter Frosting
1 *cup chopped honey-roasted peanuts*

1. Preheat oven to 350°. Combine cola and buttermilk in a 2-cup measuring cup.
2. Beat butter at low speed with an electric mixer until creamy. Gradually add sugar, beating until blended. Add eggs and vanilla; beat at low speed just until blended.
3. Combine flour and next 2 ingredients in a medium bowl. Add to butter mixture alternately with cola mixture, beginning and ending with flour mixture. Beat at low speed just until blended after each addition. Pour batter into a lightly greased 13- x 9-inch pan.
4. Bake at 350° for 30 to 35 minutes or until a wooden pick inserted in center comes out clean. Cool in pan on a wire rack 10 minutes.
5. Meanwhile, prepare Peanut Butter Frosting. Pour over warm cake. Sprinkle with chopped peanuts.

Peanut Butter Frosting

MAKES: 3 CUPS **HANDS-ON** 10 MIN.
TOTAL TIME: 10 MIN.

¼ *cup butter*
¾ *cup milk*
1 *cup creamy peanut butter*
1 *(16-oz.) package powdered sugar*
1 *tsp. vanilla extract*

Melt butter in a large saucepan over medium heat. Whisk in milk, and bring to a boil, whisking constantly. Reduce heat to low, and whisk in peanut butter until smooth. Gradually whisk in sugar until smooth; remove from heat, and whisk in vanilla. Use immediately.

PEANUT-COLA
CAKE

MENU

Slightly Sweet Tea

Buttermilk-and-Honey Chicken Kabobs with
Romesco Sauce

Hot Bacon Potato Salad with Green Beans

Grilled Jalapeño-Lime Corn on the Cob

Hot Spiced Boiled Peanuts

Blueberry Cobbler with Sugared Star
Shortcakes

FOURTH OF JULY
SHINDIG

*Independence Day is all about food, family, and fun spent outdoors. A speedy cobbler and
twists on cookout favorites make pulling off a festive celebration a snap.*

SLIGHTLY SWEET TEA

MAKES: ABOUT 2 QT. ■ **HANDS-ON TIME:** 10 MIN.
TOTAL TIME: 25 MIN.

7   green tea bags
½   cup honey
4   cups cold water
1   navel orange, cut into wedges
1   lime, cut into wedges

1. Bring 4 cups water to a boil in a medium saucepan; add tea bags. Boil 1 minute; remove from heat. Cover and steep 10 minutes. Remove and discard tea bags.
2. Stir in honey. Pour into a 2-qt. pitcher; stir in cold water and orange and lime wedges. Serve over ice.

BUTTERMILK-AND-HONEY CHICKEN KABOBS

MAKES: 6 TO 8 SERVINGS ■ **HANDS-ON TIME:** 30 MIN.
TOTAL TIME: 3 HOURS, 30 MIN., NOT INCLUDING SAUCE

¼   cup hot sauce
¼   cup tomato paste
3   Tbsp. honey
1   cup buttermilk
½   small sweet onion, grated
6   garlic cloves, minced
1   Tbsp. cracked black pepper
2¼   tsp. salt, divided
3   lb. skinned and boned chicken thighs, trimmed
      and cut into 2-inch chunks
10   (6-inch) wooden or metal skewers
Grilled lemon halves
Romesco Sauce

1. Whisk together first 3 ingredients in a large bowl until smooth; whisk in buttermilk, next 3 ingredients, and 2 tsp. salt until blended.
2. Place buttermilk mixture and chicken in a large zip-top plastic freezer bag; seal and chill 3 hours.
3. Meanwhile, soak wooden skewers in water 30 minutes. (Omit if using metal skewers.)
4. Coat cold cooking grate of grill with cooking spray, and place on grill. Preheat grill to 350° to 400° (medium-high) heat. Remove chicken from marinade, discarding marinade. Thread chicken onto skewers, leaving a ⅛-inch space between pieces; sprinkle with remaining ¼ tsp. salt.
5. Grill kabobs, covered with grill lid, 6 to 8 minutes on each side or until chicken is done. Serve with lemon halves and Romesco Sauce.

Romesco Sauce

MAKES: 1 CUP ■ **HANDS-ON TIME:** 15 MIN.
TOTAL TIME: 15 MIN.

1   (12-oz.) jar roasted red bell peppers, drained
⅓   cup chopped toasted pecans
2   garlic cloves, sliced
2   Tbsp. olive oil
1   Tbsp. red wine vinegar
½   tsp. sugar
¼   tsp. salt
⅛   tsp. ground red pepper

Process all ingredients in a food processor until smooth.

ROMESCO SAUCE

BUTTERMILK-AND-HONEY
CHICKEN KABOBS

HOT BACON POTATO SALAD WITH GREEN BEANS

MAKES: 8 SERVINGS ■ **HANDS-ON TIME:** 30 MIN.
TOTAL TIME: 30 MIN.

3   lb. fingerling potatoes, cut in half
1   (8-oz.) package haricots verts (thin green beans)
½   cup white wine vinegar
1   shallot, minced
3   Tbsp. honey
1   Tbsp. Dijon mustard
1½ tsp. table salt
1   tsp. freshly ground black pepper
½   cup olive oil
2   Tbsp. chopped fresh dill
¼   cup coarsely chopped fresh parsley
4   fully cooked bacon slices, chopped

1. Bring potatoes and water to cover to a boil in a large Dutch oven over medium-high heat, and cook 20 minutes or until tender. Drain.
2. Meanwhile, cook green beans in boiling water to cover in a medium saucepan 3 to 4 minutes or until crisp-tender. Plunge in ice water to stop the cooking process; drain.
3. Whisk together vinegar and next 5 ingredients in a medium bowl. Add oil in a slow, steady stream, whisking constantly, until smooth.
4. Pour vinegar mixture over potatoes. Just before serving, add green beans, dill, and parsley, and toss gently until blended. Sprinkle with bacon. Serve immediately, or cover and chill until ready to serve.

GRILLED JALAPEÑO-LIME CORN ON THE COB

MAKES: 8 SERVINGS ■ **HANDS-ON TIME:** 30 MIN.
TOTAL TIME: 30 MIN.

8   ears fresh corn, husks removed
Vegetable cooking spray
½   cup butter, softened
1   jalapeño pepper, seeded and minced
1   small garlic clove, pressed
1   Tbsp. lime zest
1   Tbsp. fresh lime juice
2   tsp. chopped fresh cilantro
Garnish: lime zest

1. Preheat grill to 350° to 400° (medium-high) heat. Coat corn lightly with cooking spray. Sprinkle with desired amount of table salt and freshly ground black pepper. Grill corn, covered with grill lid, 15 minutes or until golden brown, turning occasionally.
2. Meanwhile, stir together butter and next 5 ingredients. Remove corn from grill; cut into thirds. Serve corn with butter mixture.

HOT BACON POTATO SALAD WITH GREEN BEANS

GRILLED JALAPEÑO-LIME CORN ON THE COB

CREATE A DAZZLING CENTERPIECE—SMALL BURSTS OF QUEEN ANNE'S LACE ECHO THE SPARKLERS. (BE CAREFUL WHEN LIGHTING THEM!)

1. Bring all ingredients and 1 gal. water to a boil in a stockpot over high heat. Cover, reduce heat to medium-low, and cook, stirring occasionally, 4 hours or until peanuts are tender. Add water as needed to keep peanuts covered.

2. Remove from heat; let stand, covered, 1 hour.

BLUEBERRY COBBLER WITH SUGARED STAR SHORTCAKES

Look for sparkling sugar at craft stores and super-centers. If you're in a pinch, granulated sugar is a good substitute. Reduce amount to 2 teaspoons.

MAKES: 10 SERVINGS ■ **HANDS-ON TIME:** 10 MIN.
TOTAL TIME: 18 MIN.

2   *pt. fresh blueberries*
½   *cup granulated sugar*
1   *Tbsp. lemon juice*
⅛   *tsp. almond extract*
2   *(12-oz.) cans refrigerated buttermilk biscuits*
1   *Tbsp. coarse sparkling sugar*
Sweetened whipped cream

1. Preheat oven to 400°. Combine first 4 ingredients in a medium saucepan. Cook over medium-high heat 5 minutes or until bubbly and sugar dissolves. Remove from heat.

2. Separate biscuits, and flatten each into a 3½-inch circle. Cut with a 3-inch star-shaped cutter, and place on a lightly greased baking sheet; sprinkle with sparkling sugar, pressing to adhere. Bake at 400° for 8 minutes or until lightly browned.

3. Spoon blueberry mixture into 10 bowls; top with biscuits. Serve with whipped cream.

HOT SPICED BOILED PEANUTS

MAKES: ABOUT 4 CUPS ■ **HANDS-ON TIME:** 10 MIN.
TOTAL TIME: 5 HOURS, 25 MIN.

2   *lb. raw peanuts in the shell*
¾   *cup hot sauce*
⅓   *cup salt*
1   *(3-inch) piece fresh ginger, sliced*
1   *Tbsp. black peppercorns*
2   *tsp. coriander seeds*
2   *bay leaves*

BLUEBERRY COBBLER
WITH SUGARED STAR
SHORTCAKES

MENU

Cranberry-Almond Coleslaw

Broccoli Salad Dip with crudités
and pretzel rods

Slow-Cooker Beef Sliders with
Pickled Peppers

Buffalo Chicken Meatball Sliders

Whiskey Whoopie Pies

Homemade Cherry Soda

GAME DAY TAILGATE

Kick off the football season this year by showing your appreciation for the official sport of the South. Whether you're celebrating at home or hitting the road, this easy, make-ahead tailgate menu will make you the new fan favorite.

BROCCOLI SALAD DIP

CRANBERRY-ALMOND SLAW

MAKES: 8 SERVINGS ■ **HANDS-ON TIME:** 15 MIN.
TOTAL TIME: 15 MIN.

¼ cup apple cider vinegar
2 Tbsp. Dijon mustard
2 Tbsp. honey
¾ tsp. salt
¼ tsp. freshly ground pepper
¼ cup canola oil
2 (10-oz.) packages shredded coleslaw mix
1 cup chopped, smoked almonds
¾ cup sweetened dried cranberries
4 green onions, sliced
2 celery ribs, sliced

1. Whisk together first 5 ingredients. Gradually add oil in a slow, steady stream, whisking constantly until blended. Stir together coleslaw mix and next 4 ingredients in a large bowl; add vinegar mixture, tossing to coat.

Game Changer: *Make a substitution of toasted pecans for almonds. Omit the cranberries, if desired.*

BROCCOLI SALAD DIP

MAKES: 2½ CUPS ■ **HANDS-ON TIME:** 20 MIN.
TOTAL TIME: 20 MIN.

½ lb. fresh broccoli
6 oz. cream cheese, softened
⅔ cup low-fat Greek yogurt
¼ cup apple cider vinegar
2 tsp. sugar
¼ tsp. kosher salt
4 thick bacon slices, cooked and chopped
½ cup coarsely chopped cashews
½ cup (2 oz.) shredded sharp Cheddar cheese
⅓ cup minced red onion

1. Remove and discard large leaves and tough ends of stalks from broccoli. Peel and coarsely chop stems; coarsely chop florets.
2. Process cream cheese and next 4 ingredients in a food processor until smooth. Add broccoli; pulse 12 to 15 times or until finely chopped. Fold bacon and remaining ingredients into cream cheese mixture. Serve immediately, or chill up to 3 days.

BUFFALO CHICKEN
MEATBALL SLIDERS

SLOW-COOKER
BEEF SLIDERS
WITH PICKLED
PEPPERS

SLOW-COOKER BEEF SLIDERS

MAKES: 16 SERVINGS ■ **HANDS-ON TIME:** 30 MIN.
TOTAL TIME: 7 HOURS, INCLUDING PEPPERS

1   (3¼- to 3¾-lb.) boneless chuck roast, trimmed
2   tsp. kosher salt
1½ tsp. freshly ground black pepper
1   Tbsp. vegetable oil
1   medium-size sweet onion, coarsely chopped
2   carrots, coarsely chopped
4   celery ribs, coarsely chopped
2   garlic cloves
2   cups beef broth
½   cup dry red wine
4   fresh thyme sprigs
2   Tbsp. prepared horseradish
¼   cup loosely packed fresh flat-leaf parsley leaves, chopped
¼   cup chopped fresh chives
16 hearty dinner rolls, split

PICKLED PEPPERS
2   cups sliced red and yellow sweet mini bell peppers
1   cup sliced pepperoncini salad peppers
1   tsp. pepperoncini juice (from jar)
¼   cup loosely packed fresh flat-leaf parsley leaves
¼   cup thinly sliced fresh chives
1   tsp. extra virgin olive oil

1. Rub roast with salt and pepper. Cook in hot oil in a Dutch oven or large cast-iron skillet over medium-high heat 2 to 3 minutes on all sides until browned. Place roast, onion, and next 6 ingredients in a 6-qt. slow cooker.
2. Cover and cook on HIGH 6 to 8 hours or until meat is tender. Remove roast and vegetables; discard vegetables. Shred meat. Pour liquid from slow cooker through a fine wire-mesh strainer into a 4-cup measuring cup, and let stand about 15 minutes. Remove fat from cooking liquid, and discard.
3. Meanwhile, make Pickled Peppers: Stir together mini bell peppers, pepperoncini salad peppers, pepperoncini juice, parsley leaves, chives, and extra virgin olive oil in a medium bowl. Add salt and pepper to taste (makes about 3 cups).
4. Stir together shredded meat, horseradish, next 2 ingredients, and 1 cup reserved cooking liquid; discard remaining liquid. Add salt and pepper to taste. Serve on rolls with Pickled Peppers.

BUFFALO CHICKEN MEATBALL SLIDERS

MAKES: 32 SERVINGS ■ **HANDS-ON TIME:** 30 MIN.
TOTAL TIME: 1 HOUR, 45 MIN.

1   Tbsp. kosher salt
2   tsp. fennel seeds
1   tsp. black peppercorns
2   lb. ground chicken
½   cup firmly packed fresh flat-leaf parsley leaves, chopped
½   cup finely grated Parmesan cheese
½   small sweet onion, grated
2   large eggs, lightly beaten
2   garlic cloves, minced
1   Tbsp. extra virgin olive oil
1   (5-oz.) bottle Buffalo-style hot sauce
32 small rolls or buns, split
Garnishes: thinly sliced celery, fresh flat-leaf parsley leaves

BLUE CHEESE SAUCE
1   cup crumbled blue cheese
½   cup heavy cream
¼   cup sour cream
½   shallot, minced
½   tsp. firmly packed lemon zest
2   Tbsp. fresh lemon juice

1. Grind first 3 ingredients to a fine powder using a mortar and pestle or spice grinder. In a large bowl, combine chicken, next 6 ingredients, and crushed spices mixture until blended and smooth. Cover; chill 1 hour.
2. Preheat oven to 400°. Drop mixture by rounded spoonfuls onto a lightly greased aluminum foil-lined jelly-roll pan using a medium-size cookie scoop (about 1½ inches).
3. Bake at 400° for 10 to 12 minutes or until done. Meanwhile, make Blue Cheese Sauce: Process blue cheese, heavy cream, sour cream, shallot, lemon zest, and lemon juice in a food processor or blender until smooth and creamy. Season with salt and pepper to taste (makes 1½ cups). Toss meatballs with hot sauce. Serve on split rolls with Blue Cheese Sauce.

WHISKEY WHOOPIE PIES

WHISKEY WHOOPIE PIES

MAKES: 12 TO 14 SANDWICH COOKIES ■ **HANDS-ON TIME:** 45 MIN.
TOTAL TIME: 1 HOUR, 45 MIN.

1   cup granulated sugar
½   cup butter, softened
¼   tsp. table salt
1   large egg
1   large egg yolk
1¾   cups all-purpose flour
½   cup unsweetened cocoa
1   tsp. baking soda
1½   cups buttermilk
Parchment paper
¾   cup toasted chopped pecans

WHISKEY FILLING

1   (8-oz.) package cream cheese, softened
¼   cup butter, softened
2   Tbsp. whiskey
3½   cups powdered sugar

1. Preheat oven to 350°. Beat first 3 ingredients at medium speed until light and fluffy. Add egg and egg yolk; beat just until blended.
2. Sift together flour and next 2 ingredients; add to butter mixture alternately with buttermilk, beginning and ending with flour mixture. Beat at low speed just until blended after each addition. Drop batter by level spoonfuls onto parchment paper-lined baking sheets, using a medium-size cookie scoop (about 1½ inches).
3. Bake at 350° for 10 minutes. Cool on baking sheets 5 minutes; cool on wire racks completely.
4. Prepare Whiskey Filling: Beat cream cheese and next 2 ingredients at medium speed until smooth. Add powdered sugar, ½ cup at a time, beating at low speed just until blended after each addition.
5. To assemble whoopie pies, turn half of cooled cookies over, flat sides up. Dollop each with about 2 Tbsp. filling. Top with remaining cookies; press gently to spread filling to edges. Roll cookies in pecans. Serve immediately. Or place pies on a parchment paper-lined baking sheet, cover with plastic wrap, and freeze 8 to 24 hours or until firm. Store in freezer up to 3 weeks. Let stand 1 hour before serving.

HOMEMADE CHERRY SODA

MAKES: 16 SERVINGS ■ **HANDS-ON TIME:** 10 MIN.
TOTAL TIME: 3 HOURS

2   (12-oz.) packages frozen dark sweet pitted cherries
1½   cups Demerara sugar
½   cup fresh lime juice
1   (10-oz.) jar maraschino cherries, ½ cup liquid reserved
4   qt. club soda

1. Bring frozen cherries, Demerara sugar, and 1 cup water to a boil in a large saucepan over medium-high heat. Reduce heat to low; simmer, stirring occasionally, 15 to 20 minutes or until cherries are tender. Let stand 30 minutes.
2. Press mixture through a fine wire-mesh strainer into a pitcher, using back of a spoon to squeeze out juices; discard pulp.
3. Stir in lime juice and reserved liquid from jarred maraschino cherries. Chill 2 to 24 hours.
4. Stir together 3 Tbsp. cherry mixture and 1 cup club soda for each serving. Serve over ice in 16-oz. glasses.

HOMEMADE CHERRY SODA

VARIOUS PEWTER AND SILVER SERVING PIECES ARE
SCATTERED DOWN THE TABLE, SOME WITH HEAPS OF
APPLES AND OTHERS WITH FALL FOLIAGE AND
HYDRANGEAS. BOTTLES OF BRANCHES ADD HEIGHT
TO THE TABLE SETTING.

AUTUMN BOUNTY

Embrace the colors and flavors of fall with an al fresco celebration. A mix of blue-and-white china establishes the wooden table's vintage, rustic feel and complements the rich russet hues of fall leaves and piles of fresh apples.

GRILL-ROASTED CHICKEN

MAKES: 6 SERVINGS ■ **HANDS-ON TIME:** 45 MIN.
TOTAL TIME: 7 HOURS, 30 MIN.

4 cups apple juice
½ cup bourbon
¼ cup firmly packed light brown sugar
¼ cup kosher salt
1 Tbsp. cracked pepper
2 cups ice cubes
1 (5-lb.) whole chicken
Kitchen string
2 Tbsp. light brown sugar
3 Tbsp. olive oil
3 Tbsp. balsamic vinegar
5 medium-size assorted apples, quartered
1½ lb. shallots, peeled and halved
1 lb. small sweet potatoes, quartered
2 Tbsp. chopped fresh flat-leaf parsley

1. Bring apple juice to a boil in a heavy 3-qt. saucepan. Remove from heat, and stir in bourbon and next 3 ingredients, stirring until sugar and salt are dissolved. Cool completely (about 20 minutes); stir in ice.

2. If applicable, remove giblets from chicken, and reserve for another use. Place chicken and apple juice mixture in a 2-gal. zip-top plastic freezer bag; seal. Place bag in a shallow baking dish, and chill 4 hours, turning bag occasionally.

3. Remove chicken from brine, discarding brine; pat chicken dry with paper towels. Tie chicken legs together with kitchen string, and tuck chicken wingtips under.

4. Whisk together 2 Tbsp. brown sugar and next 2 ingredients in a large bowl. Add apples and next 2 ingredients, tossing to coat. Place mixture in a single layer in a lightly greased shallow roasting pan. Sprinkle with desired amount of kosher salt and freshly ground black pepper. Place chicken, breast side up, on top of apple mixture in pan.

5. Light one side of grill, heating to 350° to 400° (medium-high) heat; leave other side unlit. Place pan over unlit side, and grill, covered with grill lid, 45 minutes. Stir apple mixture. Grill, covered with grill lid, 1 hour and 15 minutes to 1 hour and 20 minutes or until a meat thermometer inserted into chicken thigh registers 165° and vegetables are tender. (Shield after 45 minutes to prevent excessive browning.) Remove from grill, cover chicken and vegetables with foil, and let stand 20 minutes. Transfer chicken to a serving platter. Toss apples and vegetables with pan juices to coat; sprinkle with parsley.

ROOT VEGETABLE MASH

Whipped, tender root vegetables and creamy roasted garlic elevate the typical mash. Any root will do.

MAKES: 8 TO 10 SERVINGS ▪ **HANDS-ON TIME:** 20 MIN.
TOTAL TIME: 1 HOUR, 5 MIN.

1   garlic bulb
1   large rutabaga (about 1 lb.), peeled and cut into
      1-inch cubes
1   lb. celery root, peeled and cut into 1-inch cubes
3   large russet potatoes (about 2½ lb.), peeled and
      quartered
¾   cup milk
¼   cup unsalted butter
1½ tsp. freshly ground black pepper
1   tsp. kosher salt
1   Tbsp. thinly sliced fresh chives (optional)

1. Preheat oven to 425°. Cut off pointed end of garlic bulb; place bulb on a piece of aluminum foil. Fold to seal. Bake 30 minutes; cool 10 minutes.
2. Meanwhile, bring rutabaga, celery root, and salted water to cover to a boil in a Dutch oven, and boil 15 minutes or until tender. Drain. Bring potatoes and salted water to cover to a boil in a 4-qt. saucepan, and boil 15 minutes or until tender. Drain. Combine rutabaga mixture and potatoes in Dutch oven.
3. Cook milk in a small saucepan over low heat 3 to 5 minutes or until thoroughly heated.
4. Add butter, next 2 ingredients, and hot milk to rutabaga mixture. Squeeze pulp from 2 roasted garlic cloves into mixture; reserve remaining garlic for another use. Mash vegetable mixture with a potato masher until light and fluffy. (Use a food processor for a silkier texture.) Add chives, if desired. Serve immediately.

FALL SALAD WITH BEETS AND APPLES

Perfectly balanced with different flavors, textures, and colors, this salad is a colorful addition to any fall spread.

MAKES: 6 TO 8 SERVINGS ▪ **HANDS-ON TIME:** 35 MIN.
TOTAL TIME: 5 HOURS

1   lb. red or yellow beets, peeled and thinly sliced
      into half moons
½   cup white balsamic vinegar
½   cup white wine vinegar
5   Tbsp. honey
2   tsp. kosher salt
½   medium-size sweet onion, cut into thin strips
½   cup extra virgin olive oil
2   Tbsp. white wine vinegar
1   tsp. spicy brown mustard
6   thick applewood-smoked bacon slices, cooked
      and crumbled
1   Gala apple (about 8 oz.), thinly sliced
3   cups firmly packed baby arugula
3   cups loosely packed frisée, torn
½   cup loosely packed fresh flat-leaf parsley leaves
¼   cup toasted chopped walnuts

1. Microwave beets and water to cover in a microwave-safe bowl at HIGH 8 to 10 minutes or until crisp-tender. Let stand 30 minutes. Drain and rinse beets.
2. Stir together white balsamic vinegar, next 3 ingredients, and 2 Tbsp. water; pour into a large zip-top plastic freezer bag. Add beets and onion. Seal and chill 4 hours.
3. Drain beets and onion, reserving ⅓ cup pickling liquid. Discard remaining liquid. Whisk together olive oil, next 2 ingredients, and reserved ⅓ cup pickling liquid until smooth. Add salt and pepper to taste. Toss together bacon, next 5 ingredients, and desired amount of dressing. Serve with beets, onions, and remaining dressing.

FALL SALAD WITH BEETS
AND APPLES

GRILL-ROASTED
CHICKEN

CANDIED ROASTED SQUASH

Score the squash flesh to create more surface area for caramelizing.

MAKES: 8 TO 12 SERVINGS   **HANDS-ON TIME:** 20 MIN.
TOTAL TIME: 45 MIN.

- 1   small halved and seeded kabocha or butternut squash
- ½   cup melted butter
- 3   Tbsp. light brown sugar

1. Preheat oven to 450°. Cut squash into 2-inch wedges; cut each wedge in half crosswise. (If using butternut, cut into smaller pieces.) Score a crisscross pattern ¼ inch deep into squash flesh, using a sharp knife.

2. Stir together melted butter and light brown sugar until sugar dissolves. Brush one-third of butter mixture over all sides of squash.

3. Place squash, flesh sides down, in a lightly greased aluminum foil-lined 15- x 10-inch jelly-roll pan. Bake at 450° for 10 minutes.

4. Turn squash over; spread with half of remaining butter mixture. Bake 12 to 14 minutes or until tender.

5. Remove from oven; increase oven temperature to broil. Brush squash with remaining butter mixture.

6. Broil 2 to 3 minutes or until well caramelized. Sprinkle with salt and pepper to taste. Serve warm.

CANDIED ROASTED SQUASH

CRANBERRY-APPLE UPSIDE-DOWN CAKE

MAKES: 8 SERVINGS   **HANDS-ON TIME:** 20 MIN.
TOTAL TIME: 1 HOUR, 15 MIN.

- ¾   cup butter, softened and divided
- ½   cup firmly packed light brown sugar
- ¼   cup honey
- 2   large Gala apples, peeled and cut into ¼-inch-thick slices
- 1   cup fresh or frozen cranberries
- 1   cup granulated sugar
- 2   large eggs
- 1½   cups all-purpose flour
- 1   tsp. baking powder
- ½   cup milk
- 1   tsp. vanilla extract

1. Preheat oven to 350°. Melt ¼ cup butter in a lightly greased 9-inch round cake pan (with sides that are at least 2 inches high) over low heat. Remove from heat. Sprinkle with brown sugar; drizzle honey over brown sugar. Arrange apple slices in concentric circles over brown sugar mixture, overlapping as needed; sprinkle with cranberries.

2. Beat granulated sugar and remaining ½ cup butter at medium speed with an electric mixer until blended. Add eggs, 1 at a time, beating until blended after each addition.

3. Stir together flour and baking powder. Add flour mixture to sugar mixture alternately with milk, beginning and ending with flour mixture. Beat at low speed just until blended after each addition. Stir in vanilla. Spoon batter over cranberries in pan.

4. Bake at 350° for 45 to 50 minutes or until a wooden pick inserted in center comes out clean. Cool in pan on a wire rack 10 minutes. Carefully run a knife around edge of cake to loosen. Invert cake onto a serving plate, spooning any topping in pan over cake.

THANKSGIVING FEAST

Enjoy a Thanksgiving menu that puts a modern flair on traditional flavors. A stunning centerpiece that groups several blue and white vessels filled with fresh cut flowers welcomes your guests to the table.

SALT-AND-PEPPER ROASTED TURKEY

With a turkey this simple and with so few ingredients, focus on the techniques that matter most. First, pat the turkey very dry, which will help it achieve a crispier skin in the oven. Then season liberally with kosher salt. Season the cavity, gently under the skin, and again on the surface of the skin to enhance the flavor from the skin to the bone.

MAKES: 8 TO 10 SERVINGS ■ **HANDS-ON TIME:** 20 MIN.
TOTAL TIME: 4 HOURS, 25 MIN.

1   (11- to 12-lb.) whole fresh turkey
⅓   cup canola oil, divided
2   Tbsp. kosher salt, divided
1   Tbsp. freshly ground black pepper, divided
Kitchen string

1. Preheat oven to 325°. Remove giblets and neck from turkey, and if desired, reserve for gravy. Rinse turkey with cold water; pat dry. Drain cavity well; pat dry. Loosen and lift skin from turkey breast without totally detaching skin. Rub 2 Tbsp. oil, 2 tsp. salt, and 1 tsp. pepper under skin and inside cavity.
2. Place turkey, breast side up, on a lightly greased roasting rack in a large roasting pan. Tie ends of legs together with kitchen string; tuck wingtips under. Brush turkey with remaining oil, and sprinkle with remaining salt and pepper.
3. Bake at 325° for 3 hours and 45 minutes to 4 hours or until a meat thermometer inserted into thigh registers 165°. Let stand 20 minutes before carving.

CRANBERRY-ORANGE RELISH

To make ahead, prepare as directed, omitting pecans. Cover and chill up to 2 days. Add pecans just before serving.

MAKES: ABOUT 4 CUPS ■ **HANDS-ON TIME:** 10 MIN.
TOTAL TIME: 10 MIN.

1   (12-oz.) package fresh or frozen cranberries, thawed
1   orange, unpeeled, seeded, and cut into 6 wedges
¾   cup chopped toasted pecans
½   cup sugar
½   cup fresh orange juice
1   Tbsp. orange liqueur (such as Grand Marnier)

Pulse cranberries in a blender or food processor 4 or 5 times or until coarsely chopped; transfer to a large bowl. Pulse orange wedges 4 or 5 times or until coarsely chopped. Stir pecans, next 3 ingredients, and oranges into cranberries. Serve relish immediately.

OLD MEETS NEW

Incorporate family pieces into your setting for a sentimental mix. Vintage transferware turkey plates top contemporary plates with blue-and-white toile patterns. On each side, antique silver utensils combine with new mother-of-pearl flatware.

CRANBERRY- ORANGE RELISH

SALT-AND-PEPPER ROASTED TURKEY

COLLARD GREENS GRATIN

Give the packaged collards an extra chop with a sharp knife for bite-size pieces.

MAKES: 6 TO 10 SERVINGS ■ HANDS-ON TIME: 35 MIN.
TOTAL TIME: 2 HOURS, 30 MIN.

5	cups heavy cream
3	garlic cloves, minced
2	cups freshly grated Parmigiano-Reggiano cheese, divided
1	tsp. cornstarch
2	(1-lb.) packages chopped collard greens
8	bacon slices, diced
2	cups chopped yellow onion
½	cup panko (Japanese breadcrumbs)
1	Tbsp. olive oil

1. Preheat oven to 350°. Bring first 2 ingredients to a boil over medium-high heat. Reduce heat to low, and simmer 30 minutes or until reduced by half. Stir in 1 cup cheese.

2. Stir together cornstarch and 1 Tbsp. water. Whisk into cream mixture until thickened.

3. Cook collards in boiling salted water to cover 5 to 7 minutes or until tender; drain and pat dry with paper towels. Cool 10 minutes; coarsely chop.

4. Cook bacon in a large skillet over medium-high heat, stirring often, 8 to 10 minutes or until crisp. Add onion, and cook 5 minutes or until tender. Stir in collard greens, and cook, stirring constantly, 3 minutes. Stir in cream mixture. Add salt and pepper to taste.

5. Pour mixture into a lightly greased 11- x 7-inch baking dish. Stir together panko, olive oil, and remaining 1 cup cheese; sprinkle over collard mixture.

6. Bake at 350° for 35 to 40 minutes or until bread-crumbs are golden brown. Let stand 5 minutes before serving.

SWEET POTATO SPOONBREAD

MAKES: 8 TO 10 SERVINGS ■ HANDS-ON TIME: 1 HOUR
TOTAL TIME: 2 HOURS

2½	cups milk
1	Tbsp. fresh thyme leaves
2	tsp. sea salt
½	tsp. ground black pepper
	Pinch of ground red pepper
1	cup plain yellow cornmeal
6	Tbsp. butter
3	medium-size sweet potatoes, baked, peeled, and mashed
5	large eggs, separated
2	tsp. baking powder

1. Preheat oven to 350°. Bring first 5 ingredients to a simmer in a 3-qt. saucepan over medium heat. Whisk cornmeal into milk mixture in a slow, steady stream. Cook, whisking constantly, 2 to 3 minutes or until mixture thickens and pulls away from bottom of pan. Remove from heat, and stir in butter. Cool 10 minutes.

2. Place potatoes in a large bowl; stir in cornmeal mixture. Stir in egg yolks and baking powder, stirring until well blended.

3. Beat egg whites with an electric mixer at high speed until soft peaks form; fold into potato mixture. Spoon batter into a well-buttered 3-qt. baking dish.

4. Bake at 350° for 40 to 45 minutes or until golden brown and puffy. (Edges will be firm and center will still be slightly soft.) Cool 10 minutes on a wire rack before serving.

GLAZED TURNIPS AND PARSNIPS

MAKES: 6 TO 8 SERVINGS ■ **HANDS-ON TIME:** 50 MIN.
TOTAL TIME: 55 MIN.

2 lb. turnips, peeled and cut into ½-inch-thick wedges
1 lb. parsnips, peeled and cut into ½-inch slices
1½ cups frozen pearl onions
2 tsp. kosher salt
3 Tbsp. cane vinegar, divided*
2 Tbsp. butter
2 Tbsp. olive oil
1 (3-inch) cinnamon stick
1 bay leaf
¼ tsp. dried crushed red pepper
¾ cup cane syrup
½ cup vegetable broth

1. Bring first 4 ingredients, 1 Tbsp. vinegar, and water to cover to a boil in a Dutch oven. Cook, stirring occasionally, 12 to 15 minutes or until vegetables are just tender; drain.
2. Cook butter and next 4 ingredients in a large skillet over medium heat, stirring constantly, 1 minute or until butter melts and spices are fragrant. Add turnip mixture; sauté 8 to 10 minutes or until lightly browned and tender. Discard bay leaf and cinnamon.
3. Stir in cane syrup, broth, and remaining 2 Tbsp. vinegar, and cook, stirring often, 8 to 10 minutes or until mixture is slightly thickened and vegetables are coated. Add salt to taste.

Apple cider vinegar may be substituted.

To make ahead, prepare recipe through Step 1. Then, spread vegetables in a single layer in a jelly-roll pan, and let cool. Cover and let stand up to 4 hours. Proceed as directed.

CARROT-CAULIFLOWER SALAD

MAKES: 8 SERVINGS ■ **HANDS-ON TIME:** 30 MIN.
TOTAL TIME: 1 HOUR, 10 MIN., INCLUDING VINAIGRETTE

2 lb. carrots, thinly sliced
2 (6-oz.) packages baby rainbow carrots, diagonally sliced
1 Tbsp. kosher salt
2 Tbsp. apple cider vinegar
1 lb. fresh cauliflower, cut into small florets
Orange Vinaigrette
1 cup loosely packed fresh flat-leaf parsley leaves
½ cup toasted walnuts, coarsely chopped
⅓ cup chopped dried dates
2 oz. feta cheese, crumbled

1. Toss together first 4 ingredients; drain in a colander 30 minutes.
2. Meanwhile, cook cauliflower in boiling salted water to cover, stirring occasionally, 1 to 2 minutes or until crisp-tender; drain. Rinse under cold running water until cool; drain.
3. Rinse carrots under cold running water; drain and pat dry. Toss together carrots, cauliflower, Orange Vinaigrette, and remaining ingredients in a large bowl. Add salt to taste. Serve immediately.

Note: *To make ahead, dress carrots and cauliflower with vinaigrette, but toss with parsley, walnuts, dates, and cheese just before serving.*

Orange Vinaigrette

MAKES: ABOUT 1 CUP ■ **HANDS-ON TIME:** 10 MIN.
TOTAL TIME: 10 MIN.

Process 1 tsp. loosely packed orange zest, ¼ cup fresh orange juice, 2 Tbsp. chopped dried dates, 1 Tbsp. finely chopped shallot, 2 Tbsp. apple cider vinegar, 1 Tbsp. honey, 1 tsp. Dijon mustard, and ½ tsp. kosher salt in blender or food processor 30 to 60 seconds or until smooth. With processor running, pour ½ cup canola oil through food chute in a slow steady stream, processing until smooth.

COLLARD GREENS
GRATIN

CARROT-CAULIFLOWER
SALAD

SWEET POTATO
SPOONBREAD

GLAZED TURNIPS
AND PARSNIPS

MOCHA-ESPRESSO CREAM PIE

MAKES: 6 TO 8 SERVINGS ■ HANDS-ON TIME: 20 MIN.
TOTAL TIME: 5 HOURS, 5 MIN.

1 (9-oz.) package chocolate wafers
½ cup finely chopped toasted pecans
⅓ cup butter, melted
⅔ cup sugar
¼ cup cornstarch
2 Tbsp. instant espresso
2 cups half-and-half
4 large egg yolks
2 oz. bittersweet chocolate baking squares, chopped
2 Tbsp. butter

COFFEE WHIPPED CREAM
2 cups heavy cream
1 Tbsp. coffee liqueur
⅓ cup sugar

1. Preheat oven to 350°. Pulse chocolate wafers in a food processor 8 to 10 times or until finely crushed. Stir together wafer crumbs, pecans, and butter. Press on bottom, up sides, and onto lip of a lightly greased 9-inch pie plate to form crust. Bake 10 minutes. Cool crust completely (about 30 minutes).

2. To make filling, whisk together sugar and next 2 ingredients in a large saucepan. Whisk together half-and-half and yolks in a large bowl. Gradually whisk egg mixture into sugar mixture; bring to a boil over medium heat, whisking constantly. Boil 1 minute, whisking constantly; remove sugar mixture from heat.

3. Microwave chocolate in a small bowl at HIGH 1½ minutes or until melted, stirring at 30-second intervals. Whisk 2 Tbsp. butter and melted chocolate into sugar mixture; spoon into prepared crust. Place plastic wrap directly onto filling (to prevent a film from forming). Chill 4 to 24 hours.

4. Make Coffee Whipped Cream: Beat heavy cream with coffee liqueur at medium-high speed with an electric mixer until foamy; gradually add sugar, beating until soft peaks form. Top pie with Coffee Whipped Cream just before serving.

SALTED CARAMEL-CHOCOLATE PECAN PIE

MAKES: 6 TO 8 SERVINGS ■ HANDS-ON TIME: 25 MIN.
TOTAL TIME: 1 HOUR, 20 MIN.

1½ cups sugar
¾ cup butter, melted
⅓ cup all-purpose flour
⅓ cup unsweetened cocoa
1 Tbsp. light corn syrup
1 tsp. vanilla extract
3 large eggs
1 cup toasted chopped pecans
1 (9-inch) unbaked deep-dish piecrust shell

SALTED CARAMEL TOPPING
¾ cup sugar
1 Tbsp. fresh lemon juice
⅓ cup heavy cream
4 Tbsp. butter
¼ tsp. table salt
2 cups toasted pecan halves
½ tsp. sea salt

1. To make filling, preheat oven to 350°. Stir together first 6 ingredients in a large bowl. Add eggs, stirring until well blended. Fold in chopped pecans. Pour mixture into pie shell.

2. Bake at 350° for 35 minutes. (Filling will be loose but will set as it cools.) Remove from oven to a wire rack.

3. Make Salted Caramel Topping: Bring ¾ cup sugar, 1 Tbsp. lemon juice, and ¼ cup water to a boil in a medium saucepan over high heat. (Do not stir.) Boil, swirling occasionally after sugar begins to change color, 8 minutes or until dark amber. (Do not walk away from the pan, as the sugar could burn quickly once it begins to change color.) Remove from heat; add cream and 4 Tbsp. butter. Stir constantly until bubbling stops and butter is incorporated (about 1 minute). Stir in table salt.

4. Arrange pecan halves on pie. Top with Salted Caramel Topping. Cool 15 minutes; sprinkle with sea salt.

SALTED CARAMEL-CHOCOLATE
PECAN PIE